Camp Matters
By the Experts

An American Camp Association Book

Harriet Lowe, Series Editor

©2007 American Camping Association. Printed in the United States. All rights reserved. No part of this book may be reproduced or transmitted in any form or by any means, electronic or mechanical, including photocopying, recording, or any information retrieval system, without permission in writing from the publisher or the American Camp Association.

Articles from *Camping Magazine* reprinted by permission of the American Camp Association, Inc.

Articles by Bob Ditter reprinted by permission of Bob Ditter.

Healthy Learning does not guarantee the URL of any internet citations used in this volume.

ISBN: 978-1-58518-029-5
Library of Congress Control Number: 2007920888
Cover design: Bean Creek Studio
Book layout: Bean Creek Studio
Front cover photo: American Camp Association

Healthy Learning
P.O. Box 1828
Monterey, CA 93942
www.healthylearning.com

American Camp Association
5000 State Rd. 67 North
Martinsville, IN 46151
www.acacamps.org

Contributors

Bob Ditter is a licensed clinical social worker specializing in child, adolescent, and family therapy. He supervises content for Bunk1.com and can be reached via e-mail at BobDitter1@aol.com or by fax at 617-572-3373.

Contents

Contributors 3
Introduction 5

*All articles in this volume were written by Bob Ditter
for his ongoing column in Camping Magazine.*

Chapter 1. Adventures With Camp Parents 7
Chapter 2. Bullies at Camp 11
Chapter 3. Campers With a Mean Streak 15
Chapter 4. Clarifying the Rules in Your House 19
Chapter 5. Communication Breakdowns 22
Chapter 6. Counting Down to Goodbye 26
Chapter 7. Dominant Girls 29
Chapter 8. Internet Blues 32
Chapter 9. Internet Challenges 36
Chapter 10. Internet Rumors 39
Chapter 11. Lesson Plans for Cabins, Bunks, and Groups 42
Chapter 12. Lessons From Summer 46
Chapter 13. Mid-Summer Letter to Staff 50
Chapter 14. More Respect 54
Chapter 15. Notes on Communication With Parents 58
Chapter 16. Respect for Authority 63
Chapter 17. Responding to Inappropriate Counselor-Camper Conduct 67
Chapter 18. Scenes From Camp 70
Chapter 19. Sensitive Issues 74
Chapter 20. Staff-to-Camper Communication Guidelines 78
Chapter 21. Taking Stock—Best Practices for Even Better Summers 82
Chapter 22. The Parent Factor 85
Chapter 23. Working With Camper Parents 88
About the American Camp Association 91

Introduction

At *Camping Magazine* it has been our pleasure over the years to introduce the camp community to a group of experts who contribute their knowledge, talent, and expertise to helping each of us address the issues that face young people, campers, staff, directors, and boards. The efforts of these capable individuals are designed to provoke thoughtful discussion surrounding the issues of the day and offer a balance of essential management and operations know-how that informs what we do and how we do it.

Whether these compilations serve as refresher courses, form the basis for staff training, fill a gap in program development, enrich an ongoing program or camp operation, or simply provide food for thought as you strive to deliver the highest quality camp experience to every individual, we believe that you will be rewarded with a renewed sense of being a part of a community that exemplifies the best in youth development practices. In every way possible, this community is firmly committed to creating summers of discovery and learning that impact every life in profound and sometimes inexplicable ways.

Part of the magic of camp is how these ideas work their way into practice and how these practices become second nature as we explore the challenges and energy that goes along with shaping the lives of the young people and staff in our charge.

To write that our contributors are the best of the best is an understatement. These articles reflect both the timeless lessons of camp and the emerging topics in the field. They are engaging, sometimes provocative, and, always, worth the price of admission.

— Harriet Lowe
Editor-in-Chief
Camping Magazine

1

Adventures With Camp Parents
by Bob Ditter

Very often, while I am visiting a camp in June or July, I not only hear about challenging camper behavior, but perplexing parent behavior as well. I decided to share one of these episodes as a way of illustrating techniques for working more effectively with camper parents. I have changed a few minor details to protect the privacy of the family and camp involved.

Rocket Boy Stages a Launch

Alec is a wiry ten-year old boy who seems to be an expert in-group mayhem, often shouting out when a counselor is talking, Alec has a mind of his own. In the summer that I caught up with him, he was rarely staying with his group, frequently running off on his own without permission or a counselor to accompany him.

His most challenging behavior, however, occurred when he was with his group mates. Alec had a very difficult time keeping his hands to himself, grabbing things from other boys when he wanted something of theirs and lashing out when he lost a game or felt "dissed" by one of his peers. When spoken to by a counselor, he complained of being "singled out" and mistreated. After about a week of his physical and verbal assaults, the other boys in Alec's group began complaining bitterly about him. Some wrote letters home to their parents and others said Alec was ruining their summer.

About 10 days into camp, while Alec was at model rocketry, he stole one of the propellant cartridges used as engines. Using some contraband matches he had snuck into camp, he tried to light the engine on the ground just outside the rocketry shack after the period was over. Luckily, the activity counselor caught him before he could do any damage to himself or anyone else, but it was Alec's reaction that most upset the staff. Rather then owning up to the fact that he had stolen the engine and endangered himself and possibly others, Alec was defiant and outraged that he was not being allowed to "have any fun." What had started out as mischievous behavior on Alec's part had quickly escalated into the mistreatment of others, eventually spiraling into behavior that was potentially dangerous behavior.

When contacted, his parents were angry and defensive. They wondered why the camp had waited so long to inform them of their son's misbehavior. It seemed to them that they were being notified at a point when the camp was ready to send Alec home, which made them feel helpless and resentful. They also claimed that Alec "never did such things at home" and questioned whether the counselors were somehow "singling (their) son out"—a tune eerily similar to the one Alec had crooned just days earlier. They also felt Alec was the "victim of poor supervision," implying that he would never have gotten his hands on that rocket engine had the rocket counselor been more watchful. Reasoning this way, it was not too much of a stretch for them to say that they felt Alec was being "punished" for the poor performance of his counselors.

Just to make things more interesting, it came out during the exchanges that ensued between the camp director and Alec's parents that Alec took a psycho-stimulant medication for attention and impulsivity while in school, a fact the parents had not previously mentioned. They had decided to take him off that medication for the summer without telling the camp.

As a camp director, were you to find yourself in this situation, you would probably be experiencing a range of reactions. You might worry about campers getting hurt by Alec. You might fear the impatience or anger of parents whose campers have already fallen prey to his aggression. You might feel defensive or angry in the face of Alec's parents' accusations. You might experience a bit of self-recrimination for not having found a way to make things "work" for this boy, and maybe even protectiveness for your staff, whose patience with the boy would be wearing thin by now as staff members become both wary and weary of Alec's conduct. With all this swirling about, how would you respond to these worried, angry, fearful parents? Let us walk through it step by step.

Take stock of your feelings.

The worst thing would be to get into a heated exchange and have your feelings get the better of you. While it is human to have feelings, it is not professional to let them have you! What you and your camp do not need is to have your feelings dictate your responses. Stall before returning that phone call if that is what it takes to get your emotions in order.

Resist the temptation to get into a blame game with the parents.

Maybe things would have been different had Alec been on his meds, but rubbing that in his parents' faces does not further your cause. Trust me, underneath it all they feel terrible. Part of their attack is an attempt to deflect the guilt they already feel. Do not fall into that trap. Take the high road. Acknowledge your mistake up front—you should have called earlier! That you may have wanted to give Alec the benefit of the doubt and time to work things out (which is true) should not distract from the sincerity of owning this mistake. Parents do not like surprises.

Likewise, do not get into an argument about their statement that "Alec never does this sort of thing at home." The best response to their claim, far fetched as it may seem to you, is to accept it at face value. It just might be that he does not act this way at home. (He just acts that way in school—thus the meds, but you will not mention that.)

"Children act very differently depending on what group or situation they are in at the time," you explain. "Alec probably doesn't behave at your holiday dinner table the same way when he's outside with his friends with no adults around." It just might be that Alec just is not ready for the kind of group-living situation that comes with camp. Some kids are more comfortable with it than others.

You will also wait for an opening to mention how hard this must be for them to hear. No parent likes to be told their child is struggling. If you have a moment when you sense they are more open, you can add that, from the sound of it, Alec has probably not had an easy go of it. If they ask you why you say this, you respond with your knowledge that kids with ADHD, which you assume Alec has been diagnosed with since he is on medication for it in school (remember, you are not a qualified diagnostician.), often have struggles others kids don't have.

Let us also consider their claim that Alec is being punished because of poor counselor performance or supervision. This argument avoids the reality that Alec seems determined to get into things that are of such danger to himself and others that he would need constant, one-on-one supervision. This is not what camp is about. Children must take some responsibility for behaving in such a way that they can be trusted. Given that Alec is sneaky, that he refuses to stay with his group, and that he is intent on breaking rules, the amount of supervision that would be required to keep him safe is not appropriate in a camp setting.

Remain firm.

Maybe you could have called them sooner. Maybe you could have thought together about better ways to manage Alec. The bottom line is that Alec has now crossed a line where you can no longer guarantee his safety or the safety of other campers. Resist the temptation to say how other parents are understandably upset about what their sons are experiencing at Alec's hands. While true, no parent is interested in what other parents or campers might think. We wish they did, but they do not, and saying so only weakens your position. It is enough that Alec has behaved in such a way where his safety and that of others cannot be assured. He simply cannot stay at camp because you cannot guarantee that safety. Next year is another year, but for now, Alec must go home.

Looking Back

Parents today are more concerned about how their children are treated by other caretakers. With all that is in the news about trusted adults mistreating children, how could they not be? Overall, parents probably should be called sooner than you might have done in the past. The point is to learn techniques like the ones I have outlined here for defusing difficult conversations while maintaining the integrity of your program. When parents are not being their "best selves" with us, it is crucial that we find ways to be "our best selves" in response. To be your best self not only serves these parents and this camper, but your reputation as a fair-minded, principled professional and the good name of camp.*

*For more techniques, go to www.ACACamps.org/handouts for a copy of the handout from Bob's opening keynote address with Jay Frankel and the True-to-Life Training Company at the 2006 National Conference in Chicago.

Bullies at Camp

by Bob Ditter

Dear Bob,

Last fall we received a phone call from a parent of one of our 12-year old female campers that was very disturbing to us. We aren't sure how to proceed.

The mother of "Lauren" claims that many of the girls systematically terrorized her daughter in her cabin. She claims Lauren was teased, ridiculed, shunned, and threatened by the other girls, all of whom were evidently spurred on by one girl in particular whom I will call "Lacey." This all came out when the mother went to reregister Lauren for next summer. She initially said she simply didn't want to come back to camp. Later, however, Lauren began to tell her mother these details. She claims Lauren is afraid to talk to us about what went on and that if Lacey comes back to camp, Lauren will not.

We checked with the counselors in that group, and they were unaware of any of this. While not our best counselors, they were reasonably responsible and involved with their campers. Any ideas about where to go from here?

— *Wondering in the Woods*

Dear Wondering,

The situation you describe fits a pattern that reveals some of the differences in the ways girls threaten or intimidate one another from the ways boys do. Girls tend to be more secretive and organized about their attacks. They often use the threat of isolation and the promise of popularity to press other girls into the service of their bullying. Girls punish other girls through relationship—banishing some, demanding loyalty from others, etc. Boys, on the other hand, shame other boys, questioning their masculinity and humiliating them through physical acts of intimidation.

It is entirely possible that Lacey could have been careful enough to organize and instigate the alleged campaign against Lauren entirely below the radar of her counselors. The sheer use of power is often the motive. I know of a coed camp in Pennsylvania where, on parents' visiting day four weeks into the summer, surprising revelations about systematic threats and harassment, much like you describe in your letter, were made to parents by their daughters, all of which had gone on right under the noses of counselors. What the girls did was wait until no adults were around to intimidate others.

Your dilemma is two-fold: 1) what to do about the current situation with Lauren and Lacey; and 2) what to do to guard against a recurrence of such a condition. The bad news is there are no simple answers; circumstances such as these are difficult to sort out.

I would encourage Lauren's mother to support Lauren in talking with you about the matter directly. First, if she has any chance of re-enrolling, she will need to get this out in the open with you. Second, if she is to recover and be less fearful, she needs to become an active participant in her own recovery. If she is like most girls, Lauren will worry about what Lacey will do if she finds out that she is "ratting" on her. She knows Lacey will deny any allegations and then really let her have it next time she has the chance. You may have to give her some assurance that, at least for now, you will not reveal that it was she that brought this to your attention.

A brave and time-consuming move would be to contact the parents of some of the other girls and, without using Lauren or Lacey's names, explain that it has come to your attention that there was a problem with some of the girls in this group feeling intimidated by other girls. Ask parents to speak with their daughters as a way of getting help to determine what actually happened so that you can restore a sense of safety to the group that may have been compromised. Stress that you do not know if their daughter was ever victimized or witnessed anything and that her comments will be kept confidential. If you take this step, it would be important to reassure parents that you are not accusing their daughter and that your goal is to get better information so you will know how to keep this sort of thing from happening in the future. (Two books you can use as references are *Best Friends, Worst Enemies*, by Michael Thompson and Catherine O'Neill Grace; and *Odd Girl Out*, by Rachel Simmons.)

Eventually, you may not be able to do what Lauren's mother wants you to do because Lacey will probably not confess, and Lauren will probably not want to confront her accused tormentor. You could offer to put Lauren in a group without Lacey, but that may not be feasible depending on the size of that age group. Even if she were in a different group, it does not guarantee that Lauren will never have contact with Lacey.

You can offer Lauren better supervision, increased vigilance of the staff (better monitoring, etc.), but again, Lauren may need help summoning the courage to report any abuse when it happens. This may not be the answer Lauren or her mother are looking for, but one focus of our work with bullying, for both boys and girls, is building resilience and resistance in kids who get targeted. Bullies, after all, choose their victims for a reason. However, even a girl with strong character will find it terribly difficult to stand up to an entire group that has been marshaled against her. That is why you should incorporate activities in your program with teen girls that help raise the awareness level of both staff and campers of this behavior.

Though it may not be "traditional camp programming," boys and girls need to have regularly scheduled, guided discussions about bullying, harassment, and other topics. Good questions are as follows:

- Have you ever been threatened or intimidated by other boys/girls?
- Have you ever seen another boy/girl be threatened or bullied?
- What actually happened? What was it like, watching it happen or having it happen to you?
- What do you think makes someone bully another kid?
- What do adults typically do about it?
- What should adults do that they are not doing now?
- What can we do to make camp a place that is safe from bullying?

The more personal sharing, the more powerful it can be in preventing such behavior happening at camp.

You will also need to educate your staff about bullying. Lead them through the same personal discussion as you would campers, using the questions above. Train them to watch for subtle signs of distress or threatening behavior in campers. Encourage staff to "hang out discreetly" (after lights out, on the porch of a cabin, etc.) to listen for covert signs of intimidation. Have all staff be mindful of their own behavior (teasing, ostracizing, humiliating) and to take a stand when they see signs of bullying so that the safety of the group is not eroded.

Dear Bob,

We had an 11-year old boy bring a hunting knife to camp last summer unbeknownst to us. About ten days into the session, he pulled it on another boy and threatened to cut him. Luckily, a counselor intervened and apprehended the knife. Both knife and boy went home. When we called his mother (parents are divorced), she was upset that her "day was ruined" by having to come get her son, and why couldn't we just keep him another three days until the end of the session. When she came to pick him up (three hours later than we had agreed on), she jumped out of her car and immediately began berating him, saying how he had "ruined her evening."

The kid was wrong. Yet, I can't help but think that his mom wasn't helping him get on the right track. Any suggestions?

— *Safe at Camp*

Dear Safe,

Several points. First, the answer to, "Can't you just keep him?" is a simple, firm, but polite, "No. I can understand how disruptive this must be for you (pause)…and…we can not guarantee your son's safety or the safety of the boys in his group."

Second, I think what you are trying to say is that this mother has made this whole incident about her. (One wonders what this boy has to do before someone realizes he needs help, not that his behavior is acceptable or should be excused.) Make it clear to the mother that when she comes to get her son you would like to meet with the two of them together. At that meeting say to her in front of him, "We all know your son's behavior was not okay, and he knows that is why he is going home. Everybody knows that when a boy does something like this, he is telling us he needs help with something. You must be as concerned about him as we are."

Even if the mother seems more concerned about her schedule or social life than her son's well-being, judging her is not helpful. It may actually be that she is overwhelmed or feels at a loss about how to raise her son on her own. Go the extra mile. Agree to speak with his guidance counselor in school or his pediatrician as a way of getting him some help. Agree to be available to speak to this person, and reiterate your concern for the boy. You might also tell him that, if he can get some help, you are open to the possibility of his returning to camp next year. He will hear your concern. Let's hope the mother does, too.

3

Campers With a Mean Streak
by Bob Ditter

Dear Bob,

Every summer we have campers who, when no one is looking, can be extremely mean to other campers. We have found this in our youngest campers as well as in older campers, both boys and girls. For example, last summer we had a boy in our "Puma" group (boys eight to nine years old) who at times was very helpful to counselors. The boy, whom I will call "Charlie," liked his counselors and was eager to volunteer and help out with cleanup and other tasks. At other times, however, he would tease, taunt, and even hit his cabin mates. One time the counselor walked into the cabin at rest hour to find him swinging a rope around, indiscriminately whipping any boy who happened to be in his way. One time a counselor caught him sneaking up behind another camper and yanking his pants down. Confronting him with his behavior always seemed to have the same result—he would initially either stare back at you blankly, as if he didn't know what you were talking about; or he would be somewhat regretful and contrite. Regardless of his reaction when spoken to, it never seemed to have a lasting impact on his behavior. What would your advice be about handling such behavior?

— *Dilemma in the Dells*

Dear Dilemma,

Many camp professionals have contacted me about mean or bullying camper behavior. Many have wondered what is causing what they see as an increase in this sort of behavior. No matter what the explanation, if you can't help Charlie control his impulses, he won't have a good experience at camp if he is constantly getting into trouble, nor will any kid near him who happens to walk into his path when he's feeling mean.

In fashioning a response to Charlie's behavior, let's start with his counselors, who are, after all, in the trenches with Charlie and are most suitably positioned to carry out the plan. They need to be coached in both the overall approach and the exact language to use with Charlie. Allow me to digress here for a moment and talk about technique.

When I meet with counselors about a challenge like Charlie, I give them a pen and a note card and have them write down what I tell them. There are two reasons I do this. First, if they do the writing, they are taking an active step in responding to Charlie, which is a good way to start counteracting any feelings of frustration or resignation they may have developed in dealing with him. By the time they finally ask for help, they are usually feeling discouraged and angry at the camper for making them feel like failures. If the counselors have "given up" on Charlie, they will not embrace the plan and it will fail. Your first job is to revive their enthusiasm and give them some hope.

The second reason I do this is that counselors, dedicated and wonderful as they may be, are also by and large not trained in the subtleties of working with campers in the way I am about to ask them to. Most counselors have a kind of trial and error, "shoot from the hip," intuitive approach. Even though it may be obvious that their approach hasn't worked, don't underestimate human tenacity. People continue to use what they are familiar with even if they know it isn't helping. I want to make sure they understand the exact language I am using and have them adopt that language and the approach it represents as closely as possible, especially since Charlie has been so successful at outsmarting everything else they've tried up to this point.

I would have the counselors speak with Charlie at a time when he is not in trouble so that he is more receptive. I would have them say the following:

1. "We've been thinking about how you've been getting along here in the cabin with the other boys, and it almost seems like there's two of you—the great Charlie that helps out and is friendly and cooperative that we love to see and the mean Charlie that can tease other campers, or say mean things, or do mean things, like the time you pulled Jacob's pants down or the time you were swinging the rope, hitting other boys." Essential points: It is important to say "it almost seems like there's two of you," and it is important to give specific examples of the "helpful, nice Charlie" and the "mean Charlie."

2. "We'd like to see more of the great Charlie that we like so much and less of the mean Charlie who hurts other people's feelings." If at this point, Charlie says he doesn't mean to hurt other boys, the counselors should respond with "maybe you don't mean to hurt anyone, Charlie, but it still happens, and we want to help you stop." If Charlie complains that he is also a victim of boys being mean to him, simply have the counselors say that when that happens he should come and tell them, and not "get even" by doing something back, which might get him into trouble. "Part of the reason we are doing this, Charlie, is to help you not get into trouble. We know you don't like it when you're in trouble, and we don't like it, either." Essential point: Children don't like getting into trouble, and the counselors are going to help him by being on his "better" side.

3. The counselors then continue as follows: "Every time we see you doing great things here at camp—helping others; doing what your counselors ask you to do; sharing with the other boys—we will let you know what a great job you are doing. And every time we see you doing or saying something mean, we're going to point it out to you." Essential point: We're going to watch you like a hawk for a few days and let you know immediately how you're doing.

4. "If after we point it out to you, you're still doing or saying mean things, then you may have to talk to the unit director or maybe even go with another group for part of a day." Essential point: We are willing to back this up with something more serious if that's what it takes.

The counselors will then have to make a concerted effort to notice when Charlie is being helpful, cooperative, or sharing and tell him, "That's the Charlie we like to see." Likewise, when the counselors see him saying something mean or teasing another camper, they will need to point it out to him, saying, "This is what we are talking about, Charlie. This is what the mean Charlie does that hurts other people's feelings and gets you into trouble." Essentially, Charlie needs more feedback, and he needs it as soon after he acts as possible.

Words Alone Won't Do the Job

Talking to Charlie and giving him more immediate feedback is only the beginning. It only provides the framework for what will invariably come next, which is that Charlie will "test" the system to see if it works. Once he does something more egregious, like slam-dunking another boy, there needs to be a consequence. This is where the unit director comes into play. Consequences need to be discussed and agreed upon with the unit director or boys head counselor beforehand, and they need to be immediate and significant. One consequence that works well with most campers is what I call "furlough." This is when a camper is separated from his or her own group and placed for part of a day in another group. For Charlie, he would move up a couple of age groups. This makes most campers uncomfortable without being punitive, and it keeps them in the program.

The unit director needs to make a careful assessment as to how many age groups ahead to send Charlie, and the counselors of the group Charlie will be moved to need to understand why Charlie is there and how he should be treated. (He will be treated with respect and will be included in the program to the degree he is capable of participating in it. He is not there to be shamed.) The other kids in the group Charlie is going to are simply told Charlie is "visiting" their group for a day. The campers in Charlie's group are told Charlie is taking a break from their group. I have found that this simple move has tremendous impact, both on "Charlie" (he gets it that you mean business) and the boys in his group, who get some time without him and have their sense of justice and fairness restored.

Another effective consequence is having Charlie talk to the unit director or head counselor while the rest of his group is at a favorite activity, goes to canteen, or some other privilege. I tend to prefer furlough as a consequence over forms of deprivation, like missing an activity, but different consequences work with varying degrees of success depending on the individual camper. In the furlough scheme, older campers are sent down to "help out" with the little kids for a day, which has equal impact as sending younger campers up a few age groups.

What About the Parents?

One element missing from this scheme is the parent connection. Given that campers have much more contact with their parents while they are at camp (emails, letters, even phone calls at some camps), and given that parents are much more involved in their children's behavior at camp, it is crucial that parents be spoken to about Charlie's behavior and the plan being devised to address it. In the next issue, I will talk about the language and the approach to use with parents and the common pitfalls most camp professionals encounter when dealing with parents about their child's behavior at camp.

4

Clarifying the Rules in Your House
by Bob Ditter

Dear Bob,

At our coed day camp this summer, we had a six-year old female camper whose parents insisted that she be allowed to swim in our camp pool without wearing a top. Their position was that there is nothing for her to hide at her age and, since six-year old boys routinely swim without wearing a top, by asking her to wear one we were enforcing a policy that was unfair to her simply because she is a girl. These are parents who are very concerned about any practice or attitude that might imply that boys are in some way superior to girls, thereby raising the possibility that she might develop a feeling of being inferior simply because she is female. While we are also very concerned about treating boys and girls the same, we are not ready to allow little girls to swim topless. The parents said they would feel obliged to pull their child from our camp if we made her wear a bathing suit top. What are your thoughts, Bob? We were clear about maintaining our policy, but not sure how to respond to these parents.

— *Perplexed at the Pool*

Dear Perplexed,

I can certainly empathize with the concern of parents who want to raise their daughters to feel as valued and to have the same rights and privileges as boys. The parents you refer to have great intentions. I wonder about their proposed solution.

While boys and girls should be treated with equal fairness and should have the same privileges, responsibilities, opportunities, and restraints, they are not anatomically or emotionally the same. Acting as if they are does a disservice to each gender. How stimulating or discomforting would it be for other children, boys or girls, to have prepubescent girls swimming topless? At what age does the policy change? What about girls who develop at different ages? For example, if a girl at age eleven has not developed breasts, should she be allowed to swim topless?

However, interesting as this question may be, it is not the one you asked me. You did not ask me about the merits of allowing younger girls to swim as their boy counterparts do. If I were to say that I think younger girls could swim topless, or that we routinely see two- and three-year olds swimming that way, so why not five- and six-year olds?—that is not the issue. However, it is not my camp, it's yours—and you've decided to stick to your policy. Given that, the question you asked is, "What do I say to these parents?"

What you simply say is—kids are well aware that different households have different rules or tolerances. Kids know that when you go visit a friend, you abide by the rules and tolerances of that household. If you don't, you may be asked to leave and/or you may not be invited back. If you disagree with the values or rules in your friend's house, then maybe your friend comes to your house instead. For example, in some households watching certain television shows or playing with certain interactive games are okay while in others it is not. In some households, there is a high level of supervision while in others there is not. In some households, there is a high tolerance for noise in others, not.

Your camp is your "household." In it, you make and maintain rules for the good of everyone there. While you may agree with an individual parent's opinion or perspective on a particular issue, you must maintain an environment that is comfortable for or fair to everyone. When children come to your "house," they are expected to abide by the policies, rules, and procedures that you have established. If they disagree, they don't have to come.

On the issue of allowing girls to swim topless, many parents allow girls to do so up to a certain age. Roughly speaking, somewhere around age three or four, society in general seems to expect that practice to change. Indeed, there are camps where children and even entire families can go and be nude—camps where such nudity is not considered sexual, provocative, or over-stimulating. From what you say, your camp is not one of them.

If other camp professionals, especially female leaders of all-girls' camps, have an opinion about allowing younger girls to swim topless, I would like to hear your opinions.

Dear Bob,

This summer we had an incident where some of our seventh grade boys had possession of some *Playboy*-type magazines, which they were caught reading during rest hour. When confronted, the three boys we caught claimed the magazines were not theirs, but were being "leased" for a fee from some older boys. After a long and bumpy process, we finally determined the owner of the magazines, who eventually admitted to running his "business" throughout the upper boys' camp. We confiscated the magazines from the boys who had them and made them call their parents, which seemed like a fitting and satisfactory response. For the boy who ran the "business," however, we felt something a little stronger was in order, since he not only brought the contraband into camp, but was exploiting others—neither of which fit the values of our camp. We therefore decided to have him go home for three days (he lives about three hours from camp).

His parents were outraged that we would send him home and actually refused to come pick him up. They told us that they had checked in with other parents who all agreed that our consequence for their son was too harsh. What do you think?

— *Pickled by Parents*

Dear Pickled,

I would ask the parents of this boy whether, when they decide on a consequence for their son when he is at home, they poll the neighborhood and put their decisions as parents to a vote. As long as you are clear beforehand that certain items are not to be brought to camp and as long as you have internally thought things through, then it is important for you to maintain what you have decided is fair. This can be a tough stance to take, especially if parents threaten to withdraw their business or try to drag other parents into their situation. However, I know that many other parents will be relieved that you are keeping standards they can count on. One of the reasons parents send their children to camp, aside from the friendships and social and emotional growth their children experience, is to have them in an environment where there are standards and where there is supervision—in many cases, a level of supervision that exceeds what they know they themselves can provide at home. Be pleasant, but be firm. If you don't keep the rules in your "house," then how do you expect your staff or campers to respect those same rules?

Communication Breakdowns

by Bob Ditter

Dear Bob,

We had a problem this summer with one of our older cabins. A group of 13-year old boys was horsing around while changing after swimming when a small group of them harassed one of the boys, who, it turns out, was new to the group. They took his bathing suit off and then began to tease him about his body. What exactly happened is not clear, as there was not a counselor in the cabin at the time.

The boy's parents were understandably upset when he told them about it in a letter home (we do not allow phone calls). The boy never said anything about it to us, so we first learned about the incident when his parents called us quite upset. Their contention is that the boys should never have been left unattended. They said that one of the reasons they chose our camp was because of a claim in our brochure about 24-hour supervision.

Bob, how do we solve the problem of privacy with older boys and girls while maintaining a high level of supervision? We do not believe older boys, who should be showing signs of increased maturity, should have counselors hovering over them 24 hours a day. Are we wrong to assume that older children would be uncomfortable and find it offensive to have counselors watching them while they change or shower? Thanks in advance for your comments.

— *Changing Times*

Dear Changing,

The problem you describe has been an issue at many camps, some of which have actually become involved in litigation over the matter of alleged substandard supervision. The standard that I have been using is that counselors do not need to be within eyesight of their campers all the time. This is especially true for older campers, who, as you point out, would feel extremely uncomfortable if counselors watched them as they changed or showered. However, counselors do need to be within earshot of their campers at all times. Had the counselor of the boys you mention been on the porch of their cabin, he would have heard the ruckus and been able to step in to prevent the boys from going too far.

I have one thought about your comment that these older boys "should be showing signs of increased maturity." While it would be nice to think that this were so, many people have made egregious errors based on what they thought "should" be true. Adolescent boys regress easily. Put them into a situation where they have to take their clothes off (changing times, showering), and the anxiety they may feel about their bodies, their development, and how they "measure up" to other boys is enough to cause a calamity. If anything, I think every counselor should assume that some boys might need more supervision during these vulnerable times, not less. Again, the way to achieve that is to have counselors within earshot of the boys, whether in the next room or just outside the changing area or showering area, so that there is privacy and coverage.

Dear Bob,

We have a problem that we have never experienced before. We recently got a call from a parent with a complaint that one of our male counselors has been instant messaging their daughter with remarks that are sexually suggestive. This parent claimed that there were other girls who had received similar messages from this counselor, who is a popular, energetic young man who has been with us for two or three years. Indeed, when we checked, there were other parents who knew about the situation, but it was also clear that they had all spoken to one another before we got to them. We did speak to some of the girls directly (with their parents listening in), and while I do not doubt their story, it was clear that some of them had been "coached" by their parents. It is difficult to know what to do about this, since I am not sure whether the parents were insinuating that we had a pedophile on our hands or not. In addition, each of the girls had erased the messages immediately, so we had no firm proof in the form of a record of these messages. What the counselor typically would say in these messages was what he would do with the girl if they were ever to be able to meet alone sometime. Again, we couldn't come up with hard evidence about what the counselor had written, and though I was a bit uncomfortable with the "group mentality" that had developed among the parents and their daughters, I was also clear in my own mind that this counselor could not be asked back to camp. However, is he a pedophile? Bob, what is my next move? As we said, the counselor in question is very popular, although there have been some concerns that he is, at times, too friendly with campers. We also once had to tell him not to give campers back rubs and not to sit female campers on his lap. The lap incident occurred on a bus which he claimed, rightly so, was crowded, so this was his attempt to make room.

— Uncertain in Cyber Space

Dear Cyber Space Sufferer,

You are not the first camp person who has told me about problems related to the Internet. Indeed, this is an area that may need more attention. Though it can be a wonderful way for staff to keep in touch with you and one another, it has been relatively unexplored in terms of potential problems. Because it is a medium that teens, staff, and parents are using more and more, especially with reference to camp, it is not surprising that some people may choose to use it unwisely.

Let us tackle the question of whether this counselor is a pedophile. The answer is that we do not know whether this young man is or has the potential to become a pedophile, but he certainly is a menace, and that is the word I would use with him and with the parents and their daughters. As to proof, there have been indications from what you have said that this young man may have some boundary issues, especially with the lap sitting and the back rubs, but if you are not accusing him of a crime, what you need is to be "comfortable" or "uncomfortable" having him in your camp—period. Though I understand your concern about the parents coaching their daughters, it is not surprising, and in some ways admirable, that the various parents have come together to protect their daughters. Could this all be a made-up prank by one of the girls? This has certainly happened before. However, to have this counselor back, who admittedly has shown you some other "red flags," would not only alienate those parents, they would waste no time spreading the word to other families. So, again, he may not be a pedophile, but you simply cannot invite him back to camp based on your comfort level alone.

The feeling you want parents to have after you speak with them is that you are responsive to their concerns about safety and that you put a lot of effort into maintaining that "safe envelope" at camp into which they entrust their daughters (and sons).

By the way, about the lap-sitting incident. My experience is that it is exactly this kind of plausible situation, the bus being too crowded, that people with poor boundaries take full advantage of. The girl sitting on his lap (and you did not indicate how old she was) could have just as easily sat on an older girl's lap, or some other younger female camper could have sat on the lap of a trusted female counselor, thus not involving him in the situation in any way.

Dear Bob,

It has come to our attention this fall that we had a problem in our boys' middle camp that we were unaware of. Evidently there was a widespread "game" which the boys supposedly called "humping"— where boys who were eleven, twelve, and thirteen would simulate intercourse using a pillow and, perhaps in one or two cases, each other. When other boys were involved it was always with clothes on, though in the cabin, the game when "played" with a pillow might occur with just underwear or a bathing suit.

When I checked this out with our supervisors, they claimed they had vaguely heard about it but never witnessed it or heard a complaint about it from a camper or counselor. When we checked with counselors, they confirmed that this had, indeed, been a regular practice by many boys and that they had felt powerless to do anything about it. Bob, you can imagine my frustration. During orientation and the rest of the summer we always tell our staff to come to us if they are feeling challenged with any camper behavior. What can we do short of resigning ourselves to the fact that there will always be things we don't know about going on in our camp? That thought frightens me.

— Missed It in Michigan

Dear Missed It,

I can well understand your frustration and I have a suggestion. Don't wait for your staff to come to you. Go to them on a regular basis, sit down with them in small groups with counselors who are working with campers in the same age range, and check in. Will there always be counselors who do not come to you or their supervisors? Yes, for many staff doing so often feels like admitting a weakness or vulnerability they do not want to admit. I find that when I check in with small groups throughout the summer, I find out volumes that I would never know about had I not asked. Not only do you create a face-saving way for staff to receive support, they support one another as a result of being in the trenches, debriefing together with an interested supervisor. Knowing what we know about staff, which is that they wish to appear competent and do not want to risk ridicule, for us to continue a practice that patently does not work (asking them to come to us) is simply not smart. In some cases, it could also lead to negative consequences for campers and camp.

6

Counting Down to Goodbye
by Bob Ditter

Dear Bob,

For many years, I have had a concern about a particular part of our program about which I would like your opinion. I operate a resident camp that has multiple sessions. We just came off an excellent summer with great staff and many happy campers. That being said, I am dissatisfied with the way we end camp with both campers and counselors. For many of our campers, the end seems very emotional, which on the one hand is reassuring—a good sign that they did, indeed, find something meaningful during their two- or three-week stay with us. On the other hand, the emotion almost seems too much for some campers. Some of our counselors seem unsure about what to do with campers at the end of camp, while I feel others get too emotionally involved with campers. Once the last group of campers has left, I feel our staff simply drifts apart. Overall, I am concerned that we do not prepare either our campers or staff well enough for saying goodbye. Do you have any suggestions about how to approach this aspect of camp life?

— *Wondering in the Woods*

Dear Wondering,

No one likes to say goodbye to good friends or good times. Because many campers and counselors have difficulty facing the end of their time together, they put off acknowledging the impending separation. Doing so can load the final day of camp with so much emotion that it can be overwhelming. While tears at the end of camp are great evidence that something important just happened, with the proper amount of time and the right activities, counselors can help campers express their feelings in ways that are both meaningful and affirming.

Though everyone handles the end of camp somewhat differently, there are some practices that the entire community should shift into as the end of camp approaches. Most camps have specific activities they save for the final days of camp, like a color war, Olympics, a banquet, or special campfire. While these activities do signal that camp is winding down, they in themselves do not help prepare children or staff for the transition that is about to occur.

It Starts at the Top

Just as you call your staff together in the days before Parent Visiting Day or some other major camp event, the process of ending a camp session should begin with a clear set of directives at a staff meeting dedicated to the topic. When this meeting happens differs depending on the length of your camp session. For a seven- or eight-week camp, it should be a full week before the end of camp. For a four-week camp, it should be about five days before the end; and for two-week sessions, it should be about three or four days before the end.

At this meeting, present the steps you want your staff to take to begin the process of leave-taking, as follows:

1. Begin a "countdown" with campers in each bunk or living unit, marking the last few days down on paper for all to see. Doing so not only helps campers prepare emotionally, but it also helps them think about exactly how they wish to spend their remaining time at camp.

2. Establish specific goals with each camper regarding the time left—finishing an art or woodshop project, passing the next level of proficiency in some activity area, going down the zip line, launching the rocket they are making, working on a cabin "yearbook," and so on. Write those goals on the "countdown" sheet. Then mark everyone's progress.

3. Do a lot of reminiscing. Recall what the first day or days of camp were like, think aloud about things campers have tried at camp for the very first time, and talk about the trips or excursions in which they have participated.

4. Engage in specific "end-of-camp rituals—making a time capsule, putting together an end-of-camp skit, making out a last will and testament, creating a picture book about their weeks at camp. Help campers write themselves a "letter from camp" that contains certain memories or positive feelings that can be mailed to them in December.

5. Provide ways for campers to talk about their best, worst, fondest, hardest, and most-rewarding moments. Circle up with campers at bedtime to talk about things like what they liked most about camp, what they will miss, what they learned about themselves, and what they can expect when they return home (family vacation, a new school, etc.).

6. Find ways to acknowledge the positive behaviors campers displayed while at camp: cooperating, helping each other, supporting friends, including others, etc. These are behaviors that are consistent with the values you are trying to teach at camp and should be validated in both spoken and written ways (like a "certificate of cooperation").

Counselors should engage in the process of saying goodbye that parallels that of the campers. Have a series of smaller unit meetings with staff to talk about the same things the campers are being encouraged to talk about—your fondest memory of camp, something new you learned about yourself, what you did this summer for the first time, how you felt you improved in your work with campers, what memories you want to be sure to hold on to, and so on. At the end, after the campers have left, have a meal with staff and do some fun reminiscing about the highlights of the season. A PowerPoint® slide show that focuses on positive staff involvement with campers and one another is a great treat at such a gathering. Consider having your staff sit in a circle and acknowledge one another for the help, support, hard work, and encouragement they offered campers and one another during the summer. This public appreciation can be one of the most-powerful ways to affirm the value of your staff and send them off with a warm glow from the summer.

Practicing these steps in deliberate ways and coaching the staff with particular activities helps to make the end of camp as meaningful and rewarding as the rest of camp. Indeed, as adults we need to give children the words and time for reflection that allows them to make sense out of their camp experience, acknowledges the growth they achieved, and helps them hold on to the gain they made while at camp.

7

Dominant Girls
by Bob Ditter

Dear Bob,

Last summer, we had a group of 13-year old girls who had the hardest time getting along with one another. Part of the problem was what we have come to call a "Queen Bee"—a strong, dominating girl who threatened and bullied the other girls and encouraged them to be mean and hurtful to one another. It was discouraging to try to talk with the girls. Normally great talkers, they seemed to clam up and deny that any problem existed. It was frustrating to know what to do. Any ideas? In addition, the more we confronted the "Queen Bee," the more she denied her actions and the more covert she became.

— *Stymied in the Sticks*

Dear Stymied,

The challenge you describe is one that many camp directors face. It is not uncommon for a strong girl or small group of strong girls to dominate a group to the point where the other girls feel threatened or uncomfortable. Extreme examples of this phenomenon can result in great physical or, more frequently, emotional harm to some girls at the bottom of the "pecking order," so it is wise to intervene. Most counselors are also stymied by this behavior and have relatively little success in confronting the behavior of the dominant girl or girls. Counselors in this position will need your help to turn the situation around.

I am not at all surprised that the girls "clammed up" when you met with them as a group. I am also not surprised that the dominant girl denied the cruelty of her actions. First of all, although most girls like to talk, since they usually experience it as an opportunity that brings about clarity, resolution, and greater closeness, they do not like to admit when their behavior is hurtful to others. Moreover, girls that are being targeted will usually not publicly accuse or "point the finger" at other girls for fear of reprisals that will occur when you and the other adults are not looking. As you said, the more you confront the dominant girl about her hurtful behavior, the more underground she will be with her behavior. Let me outline an approach that seems to offer greater success.

1. Approach the girl who is dominating the others, but do not criticize her. Instead, affirm her power ("I can see that you are a leader. I know, because the other girls listen to you.") To do this, you will have to overcome your own anger or judgment about her or what she has been doing to the others. To approach her in an angry or judgmental way will simply drive her to become more devious and sneaky in the ways she dominates others.

2. Tell this strong, dominant girl that she always has a choice about how she uses her power and goes about being a leader. She can do it in negative ways by intimidating others, or she can do it in positive ways, by taking on some responsibility or leadership role that will use her talent or ability. Tell her that you would like to help her be the strong leader that she is in ways the other girls will admire and respect. Tell her that you know that is what she wants, to be respected by the other girls, and that you would like to help her think of other ways she can do this.

3. At the same time, make it clear that being mean and threatening or putting others down is not acceptable. Clarify that you know that she may not intend to be mean or hurt others, but that this is in fact what has happened. You would like her to be the strong girl she is in ways that do not hurt others.

4. Approach the girl(s) who is (are) being victimized. If it is one girl, see what you can do to link her up with another friend. Experience tells us that girls always do better when they have at least one other friend with whom to take refuge. Be careful that this friend is not someone who tries to "protect" her from the dominate girl, as this will only antagonize the dominant girl(s). She simply needs someone she can hang out with.

5. In a separate conversation, gather together the girls who are the "silent majority"— the girls in the middle, who are either going along with what the dominant girl is dictating or who steer clear to keep from becoming targets themselves. See if they can be strengthened as a group so they can more successfully resist the orders of the dominant girl(s) to be mean. To do this, you may wish to program them so they are together as a group without the victim and without the dominant girl(s)

for a day or part of a day. Do some type of challenge activity or initiative activity where the girls can strengthen their bonds. End the activity with a discussion about being strong, supporting one another, and having a "code of conduct" where they agree not to go along with behavior that is mean to other girls.

6. Go back to the dominant girl and brainstorm ways that she can take on some true responsibility or leadership role, either in her cabin or group or in the greater camp community. This might be leading a special service, doing a skit on "Play Night," helping organize or run something in the group, etc. Involve another counselor or senior staff member if you feel this would be helpful. Determine an adult role model this girl admires who might have some positive influence on her behavior.

The point is to honor the strength in this girl rather than vilify it, and channel her attempts at being powerful into something that is productive and positive. Do not be surprised, however, if she balks at trying on a leadership role. Very often dominant girls do not feel powerful unless they are dominating a group, which is part of the problem. Helping her feel powerful and gain respect in more legitimate, acceptable ways will go a long way toward not only to correcting the problem at camp, but in permanently enhancing her self-esteem.

8

Internet Blues
by Bob Ditter

Dear Bob,

We had an upsetting situation occur between two campers during the off-season that we would like to get your thoughts about. One of our 12-year old male campers began receiving threatening emails from a screen name I cannot share with you, but which was itself a menacing moniker. The camper, whom I shall call Tom (not his real name), was being "watched" or stalked online, and in an instant message from the stalker, a threat was made on his life.

The frightened boy told his parents, who notified the police. The FBI got involved, and the screen name was traced to one of Tom's cabin mates, whom I shall call "Jim" in another state. Ironically, the boys are close friends at camp, and when confronted by the police and FBI, Jim, genuinely baffled that he had breached a line and created such a stir, was truly contrite.

My purpose in writing you has to do with the fact that Tom's parents are now refusing to send him back to camp, even though he has been with us for several years and loves the place. Jim apologized, on the phone and in writing, to both Tom and his parents. We feel that Jim, who is an otherwise helpful, outgoing, sincere camper, and who now knows that his "joke" was a terrible mistake, is only twelve and should be allowed to learn from this. We are allowing him to come back to camp, as he is much chastened by his prank. Tom's parents, on the other hand, absolutely refuse to send him back if Jim is there, even though I suspect Tom wants to return. His parents do not seem to want to budge. What can we do? Isn't it possible that a 12-year old boy can make a mistake and learn from it?

— E-dismayed

Dear E,

Your situation is the third of its kind I have heard about in the last few months. Yes, children who are otherwise essentially "good kids" are entirely capable of making huge errors in judgment, just as Jim did. The nature of IM-ing and emails exacerbates this tendency. Children, after all, often experience the Internet as a kind of pretend parallel world, separate from the kind of reality they come into contact with in the direct, personal interactions they have with friends. The virtual world simply doesn't have benefit of the nonverbal clues of communication the real world offers—facial expressions and tone of voice, for example. As a result, many kids will say things in an IM, email, or write a blog that they wouldn't dare say to another kid in person. Add to this the fact that early adolescent children are egocentric, meaning they find it hard to see the world from any vantage point other than their own, and it is easy to see why Jim thought his "joke" was harmless and might be truly baffled when confronted with the consequences of what he had done.

All of this having been said, it does not excuse the seriousness of what Jim did, and he, as other children, will only learn and widen his perspective when he is presented with the consequences of his actions. Having him apologize to Tom and his parents over the phone and in writing is a good first step. Limiting his online privileges for some time is an additional natural consequence that would reinforce the seriousness of his actions. I also think it would be helpful to Jim, Tom, and other boys at camp for Jim and Tom, with adult guidance and supervision, to discuss the entire incident with their cabin mates at camp. In this way, Jim must own up to his actions with his peers and make his amends to the community (his cabin mates) that he and Tom belong to, while helping instruct the other boys about the pitfalls of pranks on the Internet. Whether Tom's parents would accept this as an additional assurance of Jim's "reform" is not clear, but it wouldn't hurt to offer.

Aside from these steps, it is not clear what Tom's parents are objecting to. Do they think Jim "got off" too easy and that he should not be able to come back to camp? Children make mistakes and the best place for them to make amends is at the "scene of the crime." In this case, the next best place to cyberspace is camp, since it is where Tom and Jim experience their relationship, and therefore it is the place where they need to repair it. If Jim stays home, Tom may be more wounded by his friend's absence than by the original misdeed.

Dear Bob,

I happened to catch your appearance on the Family portion of the *Today Show* on NBC (July 7, 2004), where you and the mothers of different campers at different camps were talking about how camps are providing daily pictures and stories on the Internet to camp families. You mentioned that the Internet was a "great tool" for helping create a stronger "partnership" with parents. While I agree, I also know how many crazy calls we get from over-anxious parents who read too much into the look on their child's face. We had one parent call us because she found her daughter in the background of a picture, walking behind some other campers, and thought her daughter must be lonely and friendless because she couldn't see who her daughter was with. Calls like these consume time and make me wonder whether the Internet hasn't just created a whole new thing for parents to obsess about.

— *Too Much Micro-managing*

Dear Too Much,

It is true that many camps receive calls from parents who are overly concerned about their children's happiness at camp. Has the Internet created this monster? Hardly. It has simply become the new forum for parents who have always worried about their children. The parents who make these calls are the same parents who years ago called when they received an upsetting letter (or no letter at all) from their children. The only difference is that, with unrelenting news about child abductions, violence in schools, terrorism, and bullying, parents are progressively more nervous about their children's safety. The Internet did not create that anxiety; it has simply become the medium through which it is expressed. Keep your eye on the positive responses you get from your photo gallery, not the negative ones.

Dear Bob,

We recently learned that a former staff member of ours has been arrested in a sting operation involving the Internet. Apparently, this young man contacted a 15-year old boy online and arranged to meet him for sex. When he arrived, he found the 15-year old was actually an FBI agent. News of this has been on the local TV stations and in the local papers. How, if at all, should we respond to these charges? I fear that if we send a letter to parents, it may be more alarming than reassuring.

— *Fretting in the Fronds*

Dear Fretting,

I would advise you not to let your fears keep you from acting wisely. In my experience, every time a camp has contacted parents in situations such as the one you currently find yourself, parents have responded positively. Tell them you know the news has caused anxiety in many parents and reassure them about the supervision of your staff and the double coverage rule (that at your camp, children are never alone with staff members). Camp is, after all, safer than the environment at home because there are so many extra safeguards in place and so many more adults watching the children and each other. Parents will appreciate your direct approach and the openness with which you write. In the many cases I have known about where such a letter was sent, parents were only grateful for the honesty in a world where they don't expect it and often don't get it.

9

Internet Challenges
by Bob Ditter

Dear Bob,

We have a counselor-in-training (CIT) program at our coed day camp where we typically have about a dozen or so 14- and 15-year olds enrolled. Occasionally we have had a problem with CITs who are, of course, technically still campers, fraternizing with staff who may in some cases be only two or three years older than they. We experienced a new twist to this problem this summer.

Evidently, there is a website called MyJournal.com, where subscribers write fairly open, often provocative or revealing notes about themselves and others. On one of the sites, a 15-year old female (subscribers do not use their real names, but establish "profiles" about themselves) was talking about how she was being harassed by an older male counselor at our camp. She went into great detail (we looked it up once we heard about it) about his language and behavior toward her, and talked about her ambivalence about him ("He's so cute." countered by "And it kind of creeps me out.").

You can imagine our concern. Though we could surmise from the details both who the male counselor and the CIT might be, we did not know how much of what was in her blog was true, whether or not to intervene, and furthermore, how we should intervene.

Bob, what would you do?

— *Web Worried*

Dear Web,

Though there are many "new twists" brought to camp professionals by new technology, the human problems they present are as old as camp. Before I suggest some ways to proceed, let me acknowledge a new set of challenges that will undoubtedly affect camps across the country in the form of live, onsite journals or diaries.

The site you mention is one of many so called online journal sites where people can, in most cases, subscribe for free and set up their own web logs, or "blogs," as the kids call them, to share personal information, stories, experiences, etc. This is a rapidly growing phenomenon, one that is wildly popular among teens The Perseus Development Corporation, which specializes in structure for online surveys, says that over 50 percent of those with blogs are in the 13 to 19 age range. Ninety percent are 13 to 29. The most popular sites are LiveJournal, Xanga, and Blurty. Teens write in and read each others' blogs and pass out their LiveJournal addresses as readily as they do their cell-phone numbers.

Back to your dilemma. I realize the summer is over, but had you contacted me then, the following is what I would have recommended: If you feel relatively certain that you know the identity of the person whose blog is causing the concern, I would approach her discreetly and have a talk. Start by simply checking in to see how her summer is going and how she is getting along in the CIT program. In fact, I would do this as a matter of course with each CIT. First, it is simply good practice; second, it makes meeting with her less conspicuous and may help her keep her guard down.

Once you have done this "check-in," mention that an issue has come to your attention and refer generally to the blog. Tell her that you know that such online sites exist and that you are concerned about whether all the CITs feel safe at camp—including safe from any possible harassment or the feeling of being bothered. Depending on your personal relationship with your CIT, I would calmly and matter-of-factly ask her if she has seen or heard about this particular site and whether it is hers. Reassure her that you want her, like every other camper at camp, to feel safe and that, right now, all you are trying to determine is that she is safe.

Obviously, she can tell you it is her blog, or she can deny it. Even if she tells you that she is the author, you may get a denial or confirmation of the problem. (Remember that children do invent things, so remain neutral and avoid jumping to any quick conclusions.)

If she denies the blog is hers, ask if she knows whose it might be, and simply reiterate your concern that every camper feel safe at camp. Say (as if she already knows), "Of course, blogs are open for everyone and anyone to see and once word gets out, as it always does at camp, everyone will be reading this one." Coincidentally, mention that it is probably only a matter of time before the author's identity becomes known.

Muse aloud how you couldn't help but wonder whether the author of the site didn't want you to see it, since it is in such a public forum. Tell her you'd appreciate any help she could give you, and if she thinks of anything, she could always let you know. Keeping the "door open" is always a good idea with teens!

Have a sit-down with trusted members of your senior staff. Discuss whether they have detected or heard about such harassment or inappropriate behavior, and have them discretely keep an eye on the suspected "couple." Impress on everyone that there is no guilt unless there is clear evidence, but that you want to make sure everyone feels safe.

If your CIT does admit the site is hers, ask her if the situation she is describing is a real situation here at camp. If it is, you need to speak with the counselor involved and determine if there has been a breach of trust or inappropriate conduct. If so, the CIT's parents need to be informed, and the counselor needs to be fired. A mandatory report may also have to be made to the proper authority if there has been any inappropriate intimate behavior (touching, fondling, etc.). Remind your staff that they play a specific, official role as caretakers of campers, which includes CITs, and that even though there may only be a few years difference between them, CITs are still campers.

I wouldn't contact the parents of the CIT until after you have had your initial conversation with her and have gotten more information. Doing so may shatter your trust with her. Once you have more information you can determine what to say to her parents about the situation.

One last note: In all situations such as the one you describe, your relationship with your CIT, and with your staff, count for so much. The more you remain calm, exude warmth, and are open and direct, the easier it is for teens to talk with you, especially regarding sensitive situations.

10

Internet Rumors
by Bob Ditter

Dear Bob,

Last summer, one of our 13-year old campers, whom I will call "Adriana" was locked in a vicious rivalry with one of the other girls in her group. These girls have been coming to camp together for many years. We dealt with it the best we could during camp and thought it was over once camp ended.

Last fall after camp, Adriana began to circulate rumors about her rival, whom I will call "Toni," over the Internet. Adriana sent instant messages (IMs) to many of the girls in the group making various serious, damaging, and untrue allegations about Toni. She also sent anonymous emails to many other campers in what we call the "Upper Woods," which is where our teen campers live at camp. Some of these allegations were sexual in nature and all were character assaults. Adriana even sent threats to Toni under a different screen name, thinking she could not be discovered this way.

As you can imagine, the effect on Toni was devastating. Some girls in her school who also go to our camp began to shun her. A few boys who heard about the allegations made derisive comments in her presence. When we ultimately traced the emails to Adriana, she initially denied sending them. After showing our proof to her parents, she finally admitted to being the source of these hurtful rumors.

While we were appalled at this behavior, we were even more dismayed by Adriana's attitude after she admitted to her Internet harassment. She was hardly contrite and spoke about the situation as if Toni were the offender. When we heard from some of the parents of other girls in the group that their daughters were feeling uneasy about these attacks, we decided not to invite Adriana back to camp.

Bob, this is where we need your help. Adriana began to send us long emails about how we were ruining her life, how she waits all year for camp, and how important she is to the group (as she said in one of her emails to us, "I give everything I have to make camp a better place.") She argued that everyone makes mistakes and that she should be given "another chance," and that our punishment (we consider it a consequence of her own actions) is an overreaction on our part. On the one hand, we do wonder if we are being too hard. (Adriana's parents think that we are.) On the other hand, nowhere in her messages does she utter a word of concern for Toni, whom we are certain would not be back were Adriana to return to camp. What are your thoughts?

— *Chagrined in Chicago*

Dear Chagrined,

The story you relate sounds all too familiar. I have heard from several other directors (Maine, California, and Pennsylvania) with similar tales. According to *The New York Times* Sunday magazine cover story of February 17, 2002, the mean-spirited behavior of adolescent girls toward one another is commonplace and seems to peak at about 13 or 14.

Given that Adriana seems more concerned about her own well-being than she is in understanding the impact of her actions on Toni (or on the group as a whole), I would say that any attempt you make to have her apologize personally to Toni will be emotional, dramatic, and hollow. The fact that her parents apparently seem to be minimizing Adriana's actions does not bode well, either. Consider the lesson she would learn were you to have her back: make enough noise, reinvent yourself as the victim, and you can change the outcome to be what you want it to be. My concern is that if you have her back she will feel even more untouchable and have even more of a hold over the group. You must also consider the feelings of some of the other girls in the group. In fact, you are lucky to have gotten the feedback from parents of some of the other girls, as there is often a "code of silence," where girls in a group will not speak out against a female "bully" for fear of reprisals (like being "dropped" by the popular kids) that mostly go undetected by adults.

Adriana sounds like she needs to learn a life lesson the hard way by actually losing the privilege of coming back to camp. She may not learn humility, but at least she will know that sometimes, there are consequences to the choices she makes out of which she cannot charm or threaten her way. When she says that she cannot believe that you are doing this to her, you might remind her that she, indeed, did this to herself.

I believe, however, that you are not finished with this situation once you have made the decision about Adriana. What you still need to do before the summer gets under way is meet with all of the girls of the group who are returning. It would be best if this could happen before June, assuming the girls are somewhat local and you can gather them together for a meeting, but it would still be viable if it is done at the very beginning of camp this summer. You must make it clear that the purpose of the meeting is not to talk about Adriana, but for them to hear from you personally what went into your decision. I would then open things up so you can hear from them how they feel about the situation and end with a reaffirmation about what camp is all about. Have each girl set a goal for herself for the summer. Doing so will help refocus the group on the positive aspects of friendship and help everyone move forward in a positive way.

11

Lesson Plans for Cabins, Bunks, and Groups
by Bob Ditter

Anyone who has spent much time at camp knows that most activity specialists draw up lesson plans for running their periods. Well-crafted lesson plans go far beyond skill instruction and include safety protocols and rules and regulations—all geared to the age of the campers in each activity period.

Anecdotal evidence suggests this approach is highly successful. Camps, after all, routinely engage children in high-risk activities, like archery, horseback riding, ropes-course elements, technical climbing, etc., while maintaining an exceptional safety record. In addition, campers not only improve their technical or physical skills, but also increase their confidence level through a sense of achievement. It seems the structure and safety consciousness found in most activities has made them a safe environment in which campers can thrive.

Ironically, the riskiest place for campers to be is in their own cabin or bunk at resident camp or in their group at day camp.[1] While there is not necessarily a cause-and-effect relationship between safety and the use of lesson plans, it is noteworthy that most cabin/group counselors approach their work without them. My suggestion is that cabin and group counselors "take a lesson" from their colleagues in activity areas and adopt lesson planning as a legitimate way to improve the quality of the experience for their campers. To be sure, camp is not school, and it would be a mistake for the

---

[1] Inappropriate camper-to-camper and counselor-to-camper behavior account for over 50 percent of all hot line/insurance help-line calls during the summer. Most of the abusive behavior occurs in the cabin, bunk, tent, or day-camp group.

spontaneous, flow-like experience of group life at camp to be overly formalized. That being said, there is much to be gained by adding a few thoughtful routines to cabins and day-camp groups that could enhance the value children get out of camp.

First Things First

When campers first arrive, the overall goal of counselors is to help them settle in and begin making the adjustment to camp. Depending on the age of the campers, how many in the group are returning, and how many are new, the particular approach should vary.

Plan One: Getting to Know You

Objective: Connecting with each camper; increasing camper comfort level

A. Camper Groups—Youngest (with higher proportion of new campers)

- Help them settle into bunk areas or cubbies.
- Use fun activities to learn names; help them meet one another.
- Use additional activities to learn hobbies, pets, and favorite camp activities.
- Take campers on a tour of camp.
- Teach all campers a camp song or two.

B. Camper Groups—Middle (with mix of newer and returning campers)

- Help campers settle into bunks or cubbies.
- Use activities to help new and returning campers get to know one another.
- Have returning campers show newer campers around camp (supervised).
- Have returning campers teach new campers a few songs, etc.

C. Camper Groups—Oldest (largest proportion of returning campers)

- Supervise campers as they are getting settled.
- Have returning campers introduce any new members.
- Have a meeting to informally catch up on the past year (use a format where everyone answers the following questions: favorite moments from last year; something new you learned about yourself; something new you learned; some place you visited for the first time; least-favorite time or experience; etc.).
- Talk about goals for camp: What does each camper wish to accomplish?

There are several important points counselors should consider during this first "lesson period." First, be on the lookout for campers whose nonverbal language suggests that they may be feeling awkward or stressed about being away from home and in a new group. What campers do not say in words, they may say in body language or facial expressions. Second, remember boys typically connect through action first, then they can sit and talk. Girls, however, often connect first through conversation and sharing before they feel comfortable doing something together in a group. Lesson plans should take these tendencies into account. Third, new counselors working with older campers, who know one another from prior years, may find that the campers connect to one another before looking to meet them. Be patient and allow them to re-establish their friendships.

Plan Two: Group Agreements

Once campers are somewhat familiar with you as their counselor, with one another, and with the general physical layout of camp, they are ready to sit down and establish a few simple agreements. After all, they will be living together for the next several days or weeks. Having some cabin or group guidelines is a way to establish expectations about behavior and norms around what is acceptable and what is not. All campers should participate in the meeting, and its goal should be clearly explained in simple terms at the beginning: "Since we are going to be living together or spending time together for the next several days/weeks, we need some agreements about how we want to be treated and how we treat others."

Have all campers take turns suggesting agreements. Help out by writing the suggestions down, then converting them into positive statements. For example, if a camper suggests that "no one takes anyone else's 'stuff' without asking," convert that into a positive statement: "Ask before borrowing someone else's belongings." Pare the suggestions down to three, four, or five and write on a fresh poster board. Have everyone sign it and put it up in a prominent place in the cabin or cubby area. Give the set of agreements a name, like "Code of Living" or the "Panther Group Code," or "Sunflower Group Agreements." Periodically, throughout camp, use the agreements to check in with the group. How are things going? Are there new agreements that need to be established? Have campers been able to keep the agreements they made?

Plan Three: List of Firsts

One of the problems with cabin or group meetings is that counselors often have them only when there is a problem. Campers understandably resist such meetings because they come to equate them with "being in trouble." The "List of Firsts" is a great way to debrief campers at the end of each day and keep cabin or group meetings on a positive note. The "List of Firsts" is simply a large piece of paper or poster board on which counselors write whatever a camper might have done that day that they have never done before. It might be they dived off the camp diving board, tried out for a play, hit a double in baseball, learned a new dribbling technique, went down the zip line, fed the horses, or got the mail for the cabin. Counselors should talk with campers at the end of the day in a group, discussing whatever they did that was new to them. Each person takes a turn and makes out a list of discussion topics. It will grow over the days of camp and is a great way for counselors to keep abreast of what campers are doing. It also helps reinforce for campers all the things they are trying and accomplishing.

Plan Four: Public Appreciation

This is another way to keep cabin or group meetings on a positive tone while reinforcing the camp values of cooperation, helping out, etc. Once each day at the same time, preferably when all campers are together for ten minutes, sit them down and engage them in public appreciation. Here's how it works—you raise your hand if you wish to thank someone for helping you out, being nice to you, teaching you something, lending you something, showing you something new, etc. The person you recognize can be a camper or counselor. The person who is named is applauded by all the other members of the group, and then his or her name can be written on a special board or put on a slip of paper and placed into a jar for a special drawing later in the week. This activity is actually better done in somewhat larger groups, like three or four cabins or groups at once. Keep the time limit to ten minutes and simply tell those who have not had a chance to go that they can get their turn the following day.

These are just a few ideas about lesson planning for groups. Obviously, there are many other times when a lesson plan would work well. Perhaps a lesson on conflict resolution or talking things out would help campers work out their differences in more productive ways. At the end of camp, a plan for campers to share the memories they want to keep, the friends they made, and the new things they learned about themselves would be a great way to help them hold on to the growth they may not even realize they have accomplished. Again, lesson plans are not designed to take the fun out of camp but to help bring attention to all the great things camp can mean to children. Anything that helps us be even better at what we do is worth the effort.

Lessons from Summer
by Bob Ditter

While many camps and most conference centers have engagements well into the fall, if not for the entire year, much of the most-intense work occurs during the high season of summer. Taking time to reflect on these experiences while they are still fresh in our minds can provide some rich material for next summer's training and steer us toward some "best practices." It also helps to think about what I call "SCDC"—save, change, delete, and create. When you look back on orientation, your summer program, or even the way you went about your hiring, what do you want to save and do again next year? What will you keep, but change, and what do you want to delete altogether? Finally, what do you want to create to address a problem or detail that was not covered as well as you would have liked? Having visited a score of camps from May to July, I am going to share with you some notes of my own about best practices.

Staffing

Many camps in the northeast have been hiring counselors from nearby Canada with generally great results. Aside from the obvious language benefit, many camp operators report having excellent experiences with Canadian staff. First, their work ethic overall seems very strong. Second, the exchange rate currently favors them, which means that whatever you pay your Canadian workers in U.S. dollars is magnified when converted back to Canadian dollars. (It is great to be able to pay people more while not having it cost you more.) In most cases the travel and visa requirements are less complicated than those for other international staff.

Another note about staff involves new hires who have been referred to camp by former staff members. It seems that once you have a high-performing staff member and she develops a sense of caring and attachment to your camp, she takes care to refer only people who she knows will "fit in" to the culture and values of camp. I have consistently witnessed staff who have been referred by other staff to be among the best performers of the summer. If you are not "farming" your current staff for referrals in this way, you should begin doing so.

Behavior Management

This summer, I once again had the chance to see the fundamentals of managing behavior at work.

Substituting

One of the most basic notions of behavior management has to do with behavior substitution. To help a camper change an unwanted or unacceptable behavior, we need to give him or her something else to do in its place. Otherwise, even with all the best intentions, children eventually revert back to their old ways. For example, take the boy at a camp in California who was having severe, sudden temper outbursts. When the staff would finally calm him down, they would tell him how "not okay" his behavior was and how he needed to change if he wanted to stay at camp. At times, the boy would be remorseful and would promise not to do it again, but sometimes within minutes, he would be having another outburst. What the counselors did not do was give the boy an alternative to having an outburst. Once we came up with a substitution, he began to change. In the case of this particular boy, I suggested that the counselors tell him that it was okay to feel angry but not do angry things. When he retorted that no one was the boss of him, I added, "Yeah, not even you are the boss of you."

"What do you mean?" he demanded.

"Well, you certainly aren't running you. Your feelings are running you. Your feelings are the boss of you." I told him I sincerely doubted that he was the "boss of him." This irritated him, but also challenged him. Now that I had set the stage (talking is never enough with children at camp; they then need a new strategy or behavior), we created a plan where he could "prove" he was the boss of him. The plan was that, if he got really angry, he was to run to a certain place that we all agreed on (at his camp, it was a particular tree) where he could "cool off" before coming back. It was also okay for a counselor (a condition we insisted on) to approach him under the tree after a few minutes just to see if he was okay. The first time he lost his temper again (on the tennis court), the tennis specialist had to prompt him by saying, "Tree. Tree." Once he went to the tree, a counselor came over and simply told him how impressed he was that he could actually follow through. "Maybe you are the boss of you after all." the counselor wondered out loud. The boy did not stop having a temper, but he was able to manage it better, with the added benefit of being able to earn praise from the staff for better controlling himself.

Redirecting

In another case a camper's behavior was "redirected." A girl who had the annoying habit of making noises at night that kept her bunk mates up was told many times to stop. Only after giving her a "job" at night of either choosing a few songs the girls could all sing quietly together in their bunks or picking a story that could be read to all of them did she begin to comply.

A boy who wandered away from his group at day camp (or who was always far behind) was given the "job" of carrying the counselor's clipboard if he could keep up or be first. (He also got to be the leader of the line.) When, after a few successes, the other boys began to complain that they wanted to carry the clipboard or be first in line, the boy was given the "job" of choosing, along with the counselor, who would get to do his former jobs. Again, in order to have this coveted job, he had to stay with the group.

As adults, we need to make our peace with the fact that, in a camp setting, given the limitations of time and resources, our best approach is to manage behavior rather than try to change it. The advantages to all these methods are they return control of behavior to the child while giving counselors something to do besides get frustrated.

Staff Behavior

In another display of behavior-management principals, it turns out that what works with campers also works with staff. Let's take the counselor whose camp background taught him to "manage" inappropriate camper behavior by demanding, for example, that the offending child "give me twenty push-ups." It is not enough to explain to such a counselor that, even though you know he means well, push-ups and running laps and hugging trees are "not okay" methods of responding to camper behavior at your camp. Again, you must give that counselor some other way to respond to camper behavior, or he will simply go back to what he has always done.

When a camper swears, for example, that camper needs to apologize to the group. He or she may also need some suggestions about what else to do besides swear when they become angry or frustrated. If the group is challenged by too much inappropriate language, maybe the counselor needs to create a challenge for the entire group, like a "star chart," where for every day that the group goes without using certain words, they earn or keep a certain number of points. Star charts are easy to setup, and they promote positive behavior and self-awareness.

In the case of one camp in Ohio where inappropriate language was an issue with a particular group, the counselor set up a point system; each day the boys would start with fifty points. For every "swear," they lost five points. If they made it through the day without one incident of swearing, they earned a bonus of ten points. Their goal was to reach 300 points, whereupon they would get to have a special pool party for their group.

These are only a few examples of lessons learned from the busy summer months at camp. We can all learn from one another; consider sharing your summer lessons with us. Use the contact information below. Together, we make camp not only fun, but a formidable force in each camper's growth and development.

13

Mid-summer Letter to Staff
by Bob Ditter

Dear Staff,

Right about now you may be having the time of your life, enjoying the freedom of being in the outdoors in a community of good friends; or you may be wondering, "What in the world have I gotten myself into?" Whatever your particular experience at camp so far, I am writing with some thoughts about being more effective with campers and getting greater enjoyment out of your work.

Many counselors, especially those who have never been at camp before, or those who were campers for many years, wonder what all the fuss is during orientation about being a counselor. After all, how difficult can it be to hang out with a bunch of kids during the summer and have fun?

Experienced staff know better. Given the unpredictable moods of campers, the boredom of rainy days, the stress of in-fighting, the challenges of homesickness, and all the other formidable tasks that working with children brings, it is easy to see that, if you take the job seriously, being a camp counselor is hard work. Indeed, being a camp counselor is a craft—no different in many ways from being a good soccer player, cook, musician, or teacher. Sure, you can "wing it," but if you aspire to being more than a mediocre camp counselor, someone who is memorable to your campers, there are some fundamental skills and techniques you must master in order to succeed.

Survival Tip 1: Develop a "look." In fact, develop two.

Remember how, when one of your parents did not approve of something you did when you were a kid, they often shot you their "look"?

You know what I mean—that curt, disapproving glance that says, "Not here, not now, not ever." It is amazing how universal the "look" is, and how, as soon as I mention it, most counselors know exactly what I am talking about. Although the particular set of facial contortions may vary, the intent is clearly designed to stop you dead in your tracks. Judging from conversations I have had with many staff, the impact was usually pretty effective.

If you yourself don't have a "look," set about developing one now. Children are very tuned-in to nonverbal cues, and combining a disapproving "look" with the right words can be very effective. Besides, it will give you a jump on your parenting skills, even if you don't plan to need them for a few years, yet.

Tip #1 says to develop two looks. This is because you need another look that conveys your approval, not just your disapproval. This can be a gesture and a look—like a smile and a thumbs-up; or a smile and a pat on the back; or whatever comes to you naturally. That gesture and the look that goes with it will become crucial components of your communication with children, who often listen for the tone in our voice and the look on our face and not so much to the words coming from our mouth.

Survival Tip 2: Praise and reward almost always trump disapproval and criticism.

If you are like most counselors, you have a tendency to threaten campers with the loss of a privilege when you get exasperated with their behavior. Threatening children is usually not effective for several reasons. First, you often don't have the authority to follow through on some of your threats—no canteen, no going to the dance, or no going on the overnight trip. Second, threats and depriving children of privileges simply cause them to feel resentful and make them want to challenge you even more. Therefore, it backfires. I suggest praise for those campers who "do the right thing," and incentives for everyone to get things done. Create group rewards, like a special activity, in which everyone can participate. Having children work for an incentive usually works better than taking things away.

Survival Tip 3: You have two voices.

This tip is really about the feelings you may have when a camper or group of campers is engaging in behavior that is challenging your patience. The fact that you may feel like wanting to wring their necks from time to time is normal. You, of course, won't do anything of the kind, but this is where you have two voices—the one only you hear and the one you use publicly. I often tell parents that it is healthier to admit to their occasional feelings of intense anger at their children than to try to ignore those feelings, because if you don't have your feelings, they will have you. This means, however, that you need to get very skilled at knowing what you say to yourself, what to "edit," and then what to say publicly.

Survival Tip 4: There is always a "double standard" when working with children.

This reminder is true no matter where your work with children takes place, be it at camp, school, or some other child-related program. Whatever angry or negative things children may do or say to us, we simply cannot do and say negative things back to them. We are the adults in this picture. It is up to us to raise the level of a child's behavior rather than for us to lower the level of our behavior.

Survival Tip 5: Drop the emotional rope.

Of all the things I can say to you, this may be the most important and the most useful. When children challenge you, as they will inevitably do, your tendency may be to get into a kind of power struggle with them. I call this the emotional tug-of-war, with you pulling on one side saying, "Look, I'm the counselor, you have to listen to me." and a child on the other side saying any of a number of things like, "I don't make my bed at home, so I don't have to make it here." When you get into that struggle, you are actually less effective, because children are then reacting to your anger or frustration and not your good intentions.

There is a host of things children can say that may trigger us, so it is best to be aware of them and practice how to respond. The following are a few things I have heard from campers myself over the years:

- "You're not my parent…I don't have to listen to you."
    - Effective response (calmly spoken): "You're right; I'm not your parent. And everyone knows that at camp we all help clean up." (Then encourage them and move on.)
- "My father/mother is a lawyer… I can get you sued."
    - Effective response: Ignore the threat—responding to it would be picking up the emotional rope—and 1) simply, but calmly, state what you expect; 2) avoid responding to any further complaints; 3) restate what you expect; and 4) move on.

- "My parents pay a lot of money for me to come to this camp! I can do what I want."
    - Effective response (again, calmly spoken): "You and I both know (remember this phrase, you can use it over and over) that your parents didn't send you here to be wild. In addition, everybody knows that part of camp is… (fill in the blank)." Then move on.

Survival Tip 6: This is a job.

Working at camp can be tremendous fun. It can also be challenging. One of those challenges is working in close proximity with others. As in any job, you must learn to express your discontents and complaints in responsible ways. This means having the honesty to go directly to the person with whom you have the complaint, including the camp director, and expressing yourself in terms that are respectful of the other person. Doing so may be taking a risk, but it is essential if the community is to maintain trust and have integrity. You are all living too closely together to settle for anything less.

Yours in Camping,

— *Bob Ditter*

14

More Respect

by Bob Ditter

Dear Bob,

I am writing in response to the "Frustrated Director" in the article "Respect for Authority" (see Chapter 16). I liked the article and feel that it provides a valuable perspective. I have a few thoughts.

I would answer the director's question (what do I do with this kid?) more directly. From a camp director's point of view, my response would be to identify the various problems that the rude camper's behavior presents: First, of course, is the obvious rejection of the authority. It's time to make it clear to both the camper and his parents that either he "gets with the program" or he needs to leave it. The conversation with the parent needs to take place with the camper in the room so everyone is crystal clear about the camp's expectations of proper behavior.

The director also needs to make clear to the camper that there are specific consequences (clearly outlined and defined) for his unacceptable behavior along with a clear set of escalating negative consequences for future bad behavior. The second problem is the anger and frustration that must be felt by the bunk counselors who have had to endure this camper's behavior day after day. Therefore, in addition to the camper in the room when the director calls the parent, the affected counselors must be there, too. That way, by knowing the clear expectations of behavior and the future consequences of bad behavior, they can be partners in the solution (improving the camper's behavior). At the very least, their presence will allow them to understand that real action has been taken and that a clear strategy exists to effect an improvement in the camper's behavior and, of equal importance, that there is a "light at the end of the tunnel" if the camper does not improve.

Finally, the camper's bad behavior has probably either created an environment in the bunk which encourages other campers to do the same or simply makes them feel uneasy or both. In a low-key manner, the director and the counselors need to reassure the camper's bunkmates that his behavior was both not accepted and is clearly expected to improve.

I agree that our kids are being raised with too heavy a material bent. I think it's the wrong direction for many of the same reasons that you mention (in your article), but I don't necessarily agree that it promotes more rude behavior. What I do find, more often at camp, however, is that "the apple doesn't fall far from the tree." Rude, nasty, demanding parents seem to breed rude, nasty, demanding children. That corresponds well to the parent's reaction to the camp's complaints about their child's behavior.

— *Jay Jacobs, Director, Timber Lake Camps*

Dear Jay,

Thank you for your response to my column on respect for authority. With regard to your first point about addressing the director's question more directly, I don't think I could lay it out any clearer than you have. One detail I would add concerns the "low-key" conversation with the campers in his bunk. I would frame that conversation in a positive way, with the boy present, explaining to the other campers that everyone (the counselors, the division leader, etc.) is going to help the boy change the way he has been acting so that the cabin can be a happier, less-stressful place. As part of this conversation, I would have the boy offer an apology to his cabin mates for his disrespectful behavior. At the very least, I would request that he make a statement to the others committing to being more respectful in the future. Either one or both of these moves would signal to the rest of the boys (and to their counselors.) that disrespect gets taken seriously. Having to face his bunkmates also makes it clear that respect is something that affects everyone and must, therefore, be addressed in that arena.

With regard to your second point, I don't think Wendy Mogel *The Blessing of a Skinned Knee* (Penguin Books, 2001), whom I referenced in my column, or I are saying that a more materially oriented society in and of itself leads to disrespectful or rude behavior. I believe parents must demand respect from their children, and they must exemplify it. After all, respect is something children learn "through their pores." When they experience their parents and other significant adults in their lives acting in a respectful way toward others, teachers; counselors; coaches; camp directors; store keepers; relatives; even each other, they tend to adopt that same respectful behavior. Likewise, counselors who treat campers with disrespect, teasing or ignoring them; playing favorites; yelling and screaming; or preferring the company of their friends over their campers, can hardly expect respectful behavior in return. It is when counselors are caring, thoughtful, and generous with their time and attention and campers are still rude that the prescription you offer above is so necessary and useful.

Dear Bob,

We had an 11-year old boy at camp last year, I'll call him "Nathan", whom we were not sure we served very well. He had been friends with only one other boy who was very similar in his lack of maturity and social skills. Late in the summer "Josh," Nathan's friend, went back to live with his mom out-of-state and Nathan attempted to move into an older (12-13 year old) group of "normal" boys. This group had a definite pecking order and treated Nathan like they treated each other by roughhousing and teasing one another. The problem was, when they got too rough (which didn't take much—he is very slightly built and has some feminine qualities, which doesn't help endear him to his peers), he would not separate from them, but would continue to seek their attention, then go home and tell his mom and dad that he was being picked on. Their "play" didn't seem at all out of the ordinary, and we don't allow much latitude for roughhousing. Many times, I would watch him initiate contact with the older boys by teasing and "egging them on," then not be able to handle it when they came back at him. How do I help a kid like Nathan stop this cycle, and how do we train the other boys that this isn't acceptable? It was a little like watching a puppy mess around with a bigger dog and then get pounced on, you kind of think to yourself, "Hmmm, when is he going to figure this out?"

— *Jann Martin, Associate Executive Director, Decatur Family YMCA*

Dear Jann,

Perhaps the reason Nathan was not able to "figure out" his pattern with the older boys is because what he was doing is not all that apparent. One possibility is that he was attempting to "master" the social challenges of being with older boys. With Josh gone, he may simply have decided to connect with the older boys. In other words, his behavior may be an attempt (poorly executed, but well intended) to move up the social hierarchy and "toughen himself up." Indeed, this phrase, to "toughen up," is a good one to use with boys because they immediately grasp its importance. If this is the case, Nathan then has two problems: he doesn't know how to connect in any way other than by provoking the boys and he misinterprets their roughhousing as hostility rather than as an attempt to treat him as an equal. (Among boys, playful wrestling is code for, "I like you.") Understood this way, we can see that Nathan makes a valiant effort to join them at their level (one has to admit, he does a good job of getting their attention), but can't hold his own when they respond. In some ways, the older boys are just doing their part to help "toughen" Nathan up too, since from what you say their responses were within reasonable bounds.

One other possibility, however, may be that, after having lost Josh, Nathan just gave up. After all, for a boy you describe as somewhat immature, having found, then lost, a friend like Josh is quite significant. There are some boys who, when they get desperate, will make the lives of other boys miserable by being as big a pain as they can, even if it means they sacrifice themselves in the process. The only way to know is to explore with Nathan his feelings about Josh's departure. (For all we know, Nathan may blame himself for this loss.)

Nathan won't "figure it out" until you honor and validate his friendship with Josh and then assess whether his attempt at connecting with the other boys is an act of desperation or his way of trying to "move up." If it is the former, it will help enormously for him to be able to talk about it. If it is the latter, you can help him (and his parents, separately) understand his behavior as an attempt at mastery and not as a deficit. Only after pointing out the positive intention in his behavior can you explain that he either try connecting with a slightly less-rough crowd or that he get better at understanding that the boys are trying to include him and not hurt him.

The other boys may need some help understanding him, too. It is important not to make them "wrong" for responding to him the way they would any boy. If you can reach them, it might help to have one or two of the boys explain to Nathan that they don't mean him any real harm and that roughhousing is their way of being friends. If that's not his idea of what friendship is like (I suspect he and Josh interacted very differently), then that's fine, but he will need to look for boys who "do" friendship in a way in which he is more comfortable.

15

Notes on Communication With Parents
by Bob Ditter

Photo Galleries

Dear Bob,

Many camps we know now have websites where, during the summer, they post pictures on an almost daily basis of campers at various activities at camp. Colleagues who do this tell us they get many hundreds of "hits" each day during the summer as a result of this practice.

We have resisted doing this because we have wondered whether having so many pictures does not compromise that special and separate experience that we so cherish about camp. We feel that one of the strengths of camp is that it allows children to reinforce their autonomy in a safe, healthy environment. Though we want parents to know what we do, exposing that experience in such detail seems to us to dilute the independence we are trying to develop. Do you have any thoughts on this?

— *Not Convinced in North Carolina*

Dear Not Convinced,

Many camps do, indeed, have what they call "photo galleries or pages on their websites during the summer where fresh photographs of campers appear on a daily basis. These have proven to be extremely popular with parents, but your question about protecting the separateness of camp is a good one.

First, let us remember that those photographs can be reviewed and handpicked before they are put up on the site. That gives you control over what appears and what does not. I mention this not because you might have something to hide, but because a photograph seen out of context can give a misleading impression about what might actually be happening.

Remember, too, that what parents see when they view a photograph is one image frozen in time. What they do not see are the interactions that lead up to and follow that instant—those many moments that, taken altogether, make the experience at camp so special. Having photos is not like putting a video camera in a cabin or down at the waterfront, which would be intrusive.

What is also missing from the photo gallery is sound. Given that parents are still not privy to the banter and dialogue among campers and campers and staff, much of that autonomy and independence you refer to are never compromised because parents cannot hear it. I have spoken to directors whose concern about the photo gallery is precisely that it does not give an accurate or complete picture of what camp is really about. Their argument is that those "Kodak moments" are such a small part of the overall experience of camp that parents will get either an incomplete picture or, worse, a distorted one.

As long as the photographs are carefully chosen, I do not think they pose a threat to the special environment of camp. Furthermore, I do not think parents "log on" to do anything other than see their own children. These days, my sense is that parents are going to want more, not less reassurance about their children, simply because in our collective anxiety about safety and security, they, like the rest of us, want to know that "things are okay." It seems to me that the photo gallery provides a simple, convenient way for parents to get this reassurance without interfering with or intruding into that special experience we call camp.

Camp Is Calling

Dear Bob,

We train our division leaders to have a lot of phone contact with parents concerning their children. For example, we have made a promise to parents of every camper new to our camp that we would call them within the first twenty-four hours of the beginning of camp to let them know how their child is doing. We also make a call during the first three days to tell the parents something about their child's progress, like a favorite activity or new friend or special achievement, because, if we have to call later about some negative behavior, it isn't all they've heard from us. This involves a lot of work on our part, but we feel it has paid off handsomely in terms of increased parent trust and cooperation.

My question has to do with parent voicemail. We often get an answering machine or voicemail when we contact parents. I feel it is best not to leave a message. First, I am concerned that parents might think that some harm had come to their child if they hear a camp person on their voicemail without knowing what the call is about. Second, I prefer to deliver the news personally, as I think it has more of a positive impact. I believe that if we get voicemail we should not leave any message, but should call back later. What do you think?

— *Phoning in Phoenix*

Dear Phoning,

First, I want to acknowledge the tremendous commitment you have made to your parents. Given how busy those first twenty-four or seventy-two hours are at camp, contacting parents as you do is a commendable, time-intensive promise to keep. It reminds me of a practice initiated by the late Peter Kerns when he was at Nobles Day Camp here in the metropolitan Boston area years ago. Peter had his leadership team keep a logbook of all calls to parents (this would now be done by computer) so that division leaders could tell whether there were any outstanding issues before making their calls. It was also a way to establish a positive call so that the first time a parent hears from you it isn't about something problematic. So thank you for sharing your "best practice." Many camps and schools could take a lesson from you.

Before the advent of "caller ID," which is now widely used by many households, I would have agreed with your stand on leaving messages. Now, however, if a parent were to see from their caller identification log that camp had called and not left a message, you might well get the same panic you wish to avoid. This would be especially true if you had called more than once.

My suggestion is to leave a simple message, such as, "Hi, this is Camp X, and we are calling about your son/daughter, Y. He/she is fine and healthy. We were just calling because we thought you would like to know how well things are going. We will try to call you back at (leave a specific time Z)." This way you avert the possible panic that caller ID can induce without giving the details of your call in a nonpersonal way.

"Secret" Information

Dear Bob,

Recently I received a call from a parent of a camper telling me that she did not want her son in the same group as another boy who will be attending camp from their neighborhood. When I told her that we didn't honor negative requests, she asked me whether I knew that the boy had been setting fires at school and that he had also been extremely physically aggressive with other children. I was dumbfounded, since there was no indication on the boy's medical form or his application that would indicate a problem like this.

My quandary is what to do with this information, which I am not supposed to have? The behaviors described by this parent are fairly serious, yet I feel I cannot compromise the confidential nature of the woman's call. Help.

— *Pensive in Pennsylvania*

Dear Pensive,

Let me point out that, while you have cause for concern, since fire setting and physically aggressive behavior are both serious, your knowledge is currently based on hearsay. Not that I have any reason to doubt the parent who called you, but experience tells me that well-intentioned people often get only part of the entire story. Until you get more direct confirmation, you don't know what the whole truth is.

This is one of those many situations where there is no perfect solution. On the one hand, you have an obligation to protect the safety of everyone at camp, including the supposed fire setter; while, on the other hand, you don't want to stir up trouble between neighbors.

One factor you have not mentioned is what relationship you have with the parents of the boy in question. Obviously, the more you know a family, the more able you are to bring up a sensitive topic without offending them. You do this by framing your call as a concern that the boy has the most-successful summer possible. Since doing something that would further erode his relationships with peers or lead to being dispelled from camp would hardly be a "success," you tell parents that having agreements and understandings in place before the boy gets to camp may assure that he feels safe from his own impulses and that he knows people are going to be there to support him in his efforts at self-control. I would identify those people ahead of time (a counselor, a nurse, a unit director, etc.) and make them known both to the boy and to his parents. You can hardly create such a plan without knowing the boy's particular needs.

I therefore suggest you err on the side of safety and call his parents. First, ask about how he's doing and give them a chance to tell you first. If they make no disclosure, tell them you wish to "check something out with them." Again, if you frame your call as a concern for their son's well-being and they still get defensive or hostile, you then know you have nothing with which to work. You can tell them that the important issue is not how you got the information, but how to use it in a positive manner. Suggest that you and they devise a plan that will allow their son to get the most out of camp in a way everyone can be happy.

16

Respect for Authority
by Bob Ditter

Dear Bob,

Last summer we had a camper who refused to listen to his counselor. He would not help during cleanup and consistently pushed his dirty clothes under his bed. Getting him out of his cabin to activities was always a challenge, as was getting him back to the cabin or to meals afterwards. He wandered and "visited" boys in other bunks and when confronted by most any counselor, the boy, a rising fifth grader, would retort, "You're not the boss of me." His own counselor was very patient, had several "chats" with him, and tried many incentives, but the boy's behavior did not change. When we called the parents, they suspected it was something at camp, like other boys secretly teasing him or counselors mistreating him. When we reassured them this was not the case, they continued to make excuses for him.

Am I missing something? It seems to me parents find every reason to exempt their kids from responsibility, insisting always that there must be some problem we have as yet "not uncovered." When we told them that camp was about helping their son grow up, their response was, "We don't care about that; we just want him to be happy." What do you say to this, Bob? In addition, what, short of sending the boy home, can we do with such a rude and disrespectful camper?

— *Frustrated Director*

Dear Frustrated,

You have a lot of company. I hear from camp professionals and teachers around the country that children are increasingly rude, disrespectful, and inappropriate with adults. I truly believe we have a serious "epidemic of disrespect" among young people that is the result of three different, but related factors.

The first is the overselling of children. In her new book, *Born to Buy* (Scribner, 2004), Juliet Schor presents convincing evidence that youth who get caught up in the values of consumerism, expecting "the latest toy or gadget" to provide them with status and self-confidence that ultimately never materializes, become problem kids—restless, rude, miserable, and lacking inner-confidence. Marketing to children now involves focus groups with children that develop products that appeal directly to their whims, with advertisements that have infiltrated every aspect of daily life. Children wear their parents down (or buy the products themselves, without their parents' participation or approval) to get what they think they want, only to discover that great feeling of owning the "newest, latest" does not last. A cartoon in the December 13, 2004, *New Yorker* magazine shows two children chasing after their mother in a store with one child carrying a box he presumably wants his mother to buy, saying to the other child, "She'll buy it for us. We just have to stay on message."

The problem, as Schor so well documents, is that increased consumption by children only leads to disappointment, distractibility, and even depression. With so much concern on the part of parents about the threat of drugs, violence, and bullies, it is ironic that one of the most menacing dangers to our young people may be the consumerism in which they are enmeshed. Consuming simply doesn't instill in children the values of respect, grace, and gratitude. Furthermore, it suggests that the sources of strength and meaning lie outside themselves rather than within.

The second factor is the influence of the media on children, including television, the Internet, videogames, and DVDs. The phrase your fifth grade camper shouted to his counselors, "You're not the boss of me." comes directly from a popular TV show. It has become the national refrain for rude children in camps and schools throughout the country. My answer, by the way, is, "And it's clear that you are not the boss of you, either, because you're certainly not running you, your feelings are."

Children are grossly over-stimulated. They see and hear so much sexually explicit, violent, and inappropriate behavior they have come to regard as "normal," that they carry it to school, camp, and just about everywhere else they travel. One teacher at a school here in Boston told me that when she went to set a limit on some inappropriate classroom behavior by a third grader, the child mocked her in front of the other students, ran into the hallway and called back to her defiantly, "Who's your daddy." Phrased as a question, it is shouted as a statement asserting that, he, indeed, is her boss. Left uncorrected, what will this behavior look like at sixteen?

The Internet, though a blessing in many ways, has made its own contribution to the scene. One 15-year old young man that I see in therapy told me that instant messaging is a very different way of communicating, where kids will say or ask provocative things to one another online that they would never dare say to one another face-to-face. Casual sexual "hookups" are frequently arranged through Instant Messages that could never be set up in person. The overall effect is that the sense of what is appropriate and respectful is eroding.

The third and crowning factor in this flu of disrespect afflicting so many youth has to do with parents. Themselves skeptical of authority that may have been abusive, rigid, harsh, or uninvolved, many parents have done a fantastic job of educating their children about feelings without providing any sense of valid authority. As the father of one of my patients once said to me, "I don't want to be the boss." His experience with his own alcoholic father had been so distasteful that he renounced authority in general, throwing out its essential positive effects in the process of abdicating his position as a head of the house. He and his wife replaced authority with involvement, becoming overly involved in their children's lives. As a result, his children were unruly, demanding, and miserable. They complained constantly, even to the point of being ungrateful. They were exquisitely in touch with their feelings and could recite numerous reasons why they should be able to do something or not be made to do something, having become "little lawyers." To this complaining, resisting, demanding behavior this father and his wife tried talking, cajoling, and persuading, all to little or no avail.

Sound familiar? In her recent book, *The Blessing of a Skinned Knee* (Penguin Books, 2001), one of the best books I have read in the last year, Wendy Mogel, a psychologist from Los Angeles, describes how parents have instilled precious little valid authority in their children's lives—resulting in chaos, lack of internal discipline, and all the attendant problems that come with it—being self-absorbed; having low frustration tolerance; possessing little ability to rebound from a setback; and having difficulty in managing strong emotions, disappointment, etc. Written from a Jewish perspective, this book is relevant to everyone who works with children, regardless of your religious views. Want to truly give your parents a gift? Tell them to read this book, or, better, read it yourself, publish a few ideas from it in your next camp newsletter and then recommend they buy it and read it.

To me, the ultimate issue in the situation you describe is respect of authority—authority used in the broadest sense of the word. Because we as a culture have developed a suspicion of authority and have come to "question authority" (the famous slogan of the late 1960s and early 1970s), we have thrown the baby out with the bath water. Authority can be nurturing, benevolent, caring, and understanding—and still be firm. The problem is parents have developed an "either-or" outlook when it comes to authority, and have become vague and undependable, which has engendered disrespect and contempt in their own children. When someone who takes an active interest in you tells you to "stop" rude behavior, it can be a relief, even though children may at first resist and test that authority. Children will often test authority to see if they can truly count on it. When it fails, they become increasingly resentful, unruly, and undisciplined. As Mogel says in her book, "You can spend hours trying to explain and rationalize every decision, but it is your word, not your reasoning (that) matters."

I am glad that camps are presenting themselves as strong allies in youth development—offering not just fun, but growth and life learning for children. Camp can truly be a powerful force in a child's life, but without basic respect, we have no youth development. A camper who does not recognize or respect the authority of his or her counselor or director cannot learn from that adult. Indeed, certain principles of living are a kind of authority. Self-discipline, which can be thought of as the ability to say "no" to one's impulses, pays huge dividends to a child socially, academically, and emotionally.

I believe we are seeing the effects of the lack of respect for authority in children today. The behavior you describe is a symptom of this lack. When parents say they "just want their kids to be happy," assert your authority (your wisdom and experience) by saying you want them to be happy, too, and that their child will always be miserable and unhappy if they fail to recognize the good in and have respect for the kind and generous people giving them that fun—here at camp or elsewhere. Without that respect, you have nothing from which to work.

17

Responding to Inappropriate Counselor-Camper Conduct

by Bob Ditter

Dear Bob,

I received a call about an incident that took place at a resident camp this summer that I would like your thoughts about. It seems that two 21-year old male international staff members, who were off for the evening, returned to camp intoxicated. They went to a cabin, woke up the campers, and stripped one as he struggled to stop them. Once they had the camper out of his night clothes, one of the counselors held the boy down on the ground while the other counselor removed his own shorts and underwear and squatted over the boy's face, touching the body of the camper with his bare end—a move that was later referred to as "tea bagging." The campers complained. The camper who had been singled out was visibly and understandably upset.

My concerns have to do with how the camp responded to the incident. The counselors were fired, and the parents of the involved campers were all called. The parents of the boys who were not stripped and touched were upset, but satisfied that the counselors had been fired and that their sons seemed okay. Surprisingly, the parents of the boy who was singled out reacted minimally, evidently seeing the incident as a "camp prank." They, too, were satisfied with the resolution. The camp returned to business as usual and a decision was made that the less said, the better.

Bob, what are your thoughts about this "resolution?"

— *Norman E. Friedman, Director AM Skier's Safety Underwriter's Department*

Dear Norman,

Thank you for sharing what I am sure most camp professionals would agree is an egregious case of counselor abuse. My first and greatest concern is for the male camper who was victimized by these two staff. Regardless of the reported reaction of his parents, this young man was singled out, violated, and humiliated in front of his peers. Having treated many child victims of abuse, I imagine this boy will have lasting, profound emotional difficulties unless he gets some professional help. The less than supportive response of his parents may even contribute to his upset, as he must be wondering why it was they did not acknowledge his pain and suffering and come to his aid. If he is typical of the many boys I have treated who have been victimized in similar ways, what he will wrestle with the rest of his life is why he, of all the boys in the group, was singled out for such treatment. Without help, he will continue to agonize over his own imagined culpability, with possible devastating effects.

For the sake of the boy, therefore, as well as for the well-being of the other boys in the group who witnessed this scene and who were also "violated," this situation needs a stronger response than the one you outline in your letter. Though it is understandable that the owners-directors involved would be tempted to "want the problem to go away," one would hope their concern for the boy and their sense of professionalism would prevail. Indeed, were a lawsuit to be filed at a later date against the camp for neglect, the fact that the camp minimized the problem and did not take the proper steps to address the situation would be a major factor against them.

Here are the steps I would recommend:

1. Each boy in the group should be initially interviewed to gain a rudimentary grasp on the chain of events (this done while the counselors are isolated from other campers). I would actually have each boy write his own account out on paper and follow up with a face-to-face interview. Each boy should be interviewed separately, and there should always be another adult in the room while this takes place. Make sure the person speaking with the boys is comfortable with this role, and take steps to make sure the boys feel cared for.

2. The boys must also be spoken to as a group and an appeal made to "keep this private" while you follow up. Tell them that the boy who was targeted needs their help maintaining his privacy and dignity. You might have them involved in a group activity for a few hours in the morning away from the rest of the camp while your process continues. The boys must also be told that their parents will be called and that they are welcome to speak with their parents if they so desire.

3. I would summon the staff as a whole right before or after breakfast and tell them you need their help. I would tell them that an incident had occurred (without giving too many details) and ask their help in quelling rumors. I would ask the staff to help keep camp focused on camp and not on this incident.

4. The police need to be called, as does the agency responsible for bringing these counselors into the country and the child-protective agency in the state the camp is located in. It is never the jurisdiction of the camp owner or director to decide whether counselors who have perpetrated abuse can be freed or not. The only people charged to make that judgment are the police or the child-protective agency. To violate this principle is unethical and could lead to criminal charges against the camp (for not following the mandated reporter law) and open them to civil prosecution at a later date.

5. As for the boys, I would have a trained professional sit with them to debrief and assess the level of trauma they experienced. Any parent who wished to visit with their son by phone or personally would be allowed to do so, and I would offer this not only to the parents, but to the boys as well. (I would work with the parents to encourage the boys to stay at camp, since the best prognosis would be for them to finish their session and, with support, move on.)

6. I would insist the parents of the boy who was singled out for "special treatment" come to camp and speak with their boy. Once there, I would recommend that a professional therapist be located to do an assessment of the boy as soon as possible. Whether the boy would go home or not would depend on his state of mind after visiting with his parents. It could be that he could finish out his session, then get the evaluation; or get the evaluation and return in a day or two to camp.

7. I would make sure to check in with trusted members of the staff to see what the level of rumor was and to decide whether a letter sent to all parents a bit later in the summer might be necessary. (Remember that the identity of the boy must be protected, for his sake and the sake of any other camper who might be hurt in the future.)

8. I would review the policy regarding curfew and checking staff in. Did the camp have a policy in place? If not, they need one. If so, it was not enforced properly (those counselors should never have made it back to the bunk). I would want to know where the breakdown occurred.

9. If possible, I would have the two counselors write an apology to the camper, to the group, and to the entire staff. They would need to take full responsibility for their wrongful behavior. Whether or not they would comply (especially if it could later be used against them) is not clear, but it would be a great help, especially for the boy who was victimized.

This is the short list, but a good start. I would reiterate a piece of advice I have heard you give many camps over the years, Norman, which is to form a "crisis-response team" composed of trusted senior administrators, perhaps a trusted colleague, a lawyer, a mental-health professional, and a public relations person, and I would be in touch with this team as I moved through the above process. These steps and the professionalism they represent are the kinds of practices that all camp professionals must learn as we all make our camps safer places for children.

18

Scenes from Camp
by Bob Ditter

June and July are travel months for me. Twenty days each month, I can be found in a camp somewhere in the United States listening to the tales of counselors dealing valiantly with challenging camper behavior. I have chosen to share a couple of episodes from last summer with the hope that you, intrepid reader, will find some elements of them familiar and therefore useful. The names of the campers and some of the details of their situations have been changed to protect their privacy.

Gaining Respect

Damian is a 13-year old boy in his first year at a coed resident camp that has one eight-week session. He is diagnosed with Tourette's syndrome, which for Damian manifests itself as eye and facial tics (erratic, involuntary sudden movements) and some vocal tics, mostly growling or clearing his throat or sniffing the air through his nose. These behaviors often increase in frequency, intensity, and duration when Damian is anxious or stressed about something, or when he is in a new situation. While Damian has been teased in school for some of his behavior, which is largely beyond his control, the boys at camp do not tease him for anything related to his tics. Once they had a clear understanding of his condition and the fact that it was not something he could easily control, an explanation that was given to his cabin group in his presence on the first day of camp, they "cut him a lot of slack" and never bothered him about it.

What they did bother him about was his bragging. Once, while preparing to play baseball with his group, as the boys were lobbying for what field position they wanted to play, Damian spoke forcefully and convincingly about why he should be allowed to pitch. He claimed that he had had a lot of experience and was the best they had ever seen. After a miserable outing, it came out that he had never pitched before in his life. The boys on his team were furious with him. Had he not been so vocal about his prowess as a pitcher, they would not have been so let down by either his performance (which cost them the game) or the fact that this was his first attempt at it. Had this been an isolated incident, one could see how Damian might have just wanted to try something he had never done before (camp after all is a great place to try new things). For Damian, however, bragging was a sport in itself.

Damian bragged about places he had traveled to, stars he had met, achievements he had accumulated, and skills he had perfected—all of which were either grossly exaggerated or wholly untrue. It got to the point that whatever he said, the other boys, because they could never trust him, would ridicule him or react with hostility. They were so offended by what they considered lies that they began to tease him mercilessly. During times like this, Damian would lash out physically at his tormentors who in turn felt that they were justified in their reactions because his claims were so outrageous. Of course, their hostility did nothing to sway Damian from his habit, but only brought out his aggression. You and I might think, hmmm, here is a kid who, given what he has been through, is understandably insecure about himself and therefore tries to "build himself up" by embellishing things about himself. We might even be right. The question is, as it always is at camp, what can be done about it?

It was decided that I would talk with Damian myself. After securing permission from his parents to meet with him one-on-one, I sat down with him. I made it clear that I knew about Tourette's, which I had seen several people in my practice who had had it, and then also told him that I knew his camp friends had been giving him a hard time. I asked him to describe what it was they had been doing that had been upsetting him so and just listened for a while. I then asked him if he had any idea what it was that made the other boys taunt him as they did. I did not expect him to give me an answer that accounted for his part of the problem and he didn't. This, of course, was all just "setting the table." I was now ready to serve up the main course.

"So, Damian," I started, "I can see you are truly bothered by what the other boys sometimes do. In fact, it has gotten you so riled up that you've been in danger of getting into trouble over it. I don't think you want that to happen. In fact, I think you'd like the boys to treat you differently or you wouldn't be here talking to me." He agreed.

"So, let me ask you…if there was one thing you could do to change things, would you be willing to do it?"

"Sure," he said. "But, I guess it depends on what it is."

"Good answer." I replied. "How about this," I continued. "How about if before you do or say something to the other boys, you stop first and ask yourself one question. Would you be willing to try that?"

"Um, I guess so. What's the question?" he asked.

"Will what you are about to do or say make the other boys respect you more, or respect you less. For example, will lashing out at them make them respect you more, or will it make them respect you less. I don't want you to answer me now; I just want you to ask yourself that question each and every time you go to do or say something in front of the other boys.

"See, I think what you really want is for the boys to respect you. I think you want it so badly that you've sometimes exaggerated things you've said to try to get it. In addition, I have a hunch you can get it, but only if you ask yourself that question first. For example, if you keep playing or keep working at something even though you are feeling hurt or angry, would that make the other boys respect you more, or respect you less?"

Had Damian been 11-years old and not 13, this approach might not have worked. Had he not been in pain, it most likely wouldn't have worked. Had respect not been a key issue for him (for all boys his age), I would have been off the mark. However, he was 13; he was in pain; he was hungry for the other boys to respect him; and I was able to talk to him in a way that was at once direct, but respectful. And it worked. In fact, he was able to make quite a dramatic turnaround. The camp director has the post camp letter from his grateful mother to prove it.

One Thing at a Time

Marissa is an eight-year old, first-time camper who is driving her counselors crazy. It's her specialty. "We tell her three things to do," one counselor tells me, "like, 'put on your shoes, make your bed, and put your dirty laundry in your laundry bag.' She smiles and agrees, but within seconds, she's off doing something else. I feel like calling her parents and saying, 'You have the most ADD kid I've ever seen.'"

I momentarily stifled my impulse to point out that...

1. they were not qualified to make that judgment and hand her a diagnosis; and
2. that her distractibility could just as easily been because of a number of things, including immaturity, adjusting to the entirely new and very stimulating situation of suddenly having eight or more "sisters" to share a room with (the season-long pajama party.) or not having her doting parents do everything for her (like lay out her clothes, pick up her things, and so on).

But I checked myself.

"Let's try something else," I said in quietly confident way. "Something simple and easy to do that we can build on. I'd like you both to follow exactly the same format for a couple of days and then we'll see about tweaking it.

"First, tell her one thing and only one thing to do, like, 'put on your shoes.' Have her repeat that one thing back to you. Send her off to do it while you attend to other things, but first, instruct her to come back to you and tell you when she's finished that one thing. Praise her when she comes back and announces that she's done her one thing. Don't go overboard, a simple, 'Good job, Marissa. That's great.' will suffice. Then, give her a second thing to do with the same instructions. Then a third, etc. One direction at a time. It may be somewhat tedious for you both at first, but…

1. you can 'tag team' her so one of you isn't always the one having to work with her;
2. you can continue to go about your business while she's doing her one thing;
3. the praise she will get is like built-in sugar—she'll come back for more; and
4. after a couple of days, you can start experimenting with giving her two things to do in a row and save your praise for when she's reported back to you that she's done both things."

Had Marissa been twelve or 13, this would not have worked. Had she not been eager to feel successful and win the approval of her counselors, something generally true of younger campers, it might not have worked. It did work, which might mean we have discovered a "cure" for ADD after all.

19

Sensitive Issues
by Bob Ditter

Dear Bob,

I am a director at a Christian camp in California. This summer one of my counselors was challenged with a cabin of ten 13-year old boys who were very interested in talking about and asking questions about sex and girls—not unusual for boys this age, obviously. As you know, however, my camp is a Christian organization, and we generally do not consider sex and sexuality the kind of discussion that our staff would bring up to the campers. I also know enough about 13-year old boys to know that they will invariably bring the topic up with a counselor.

I have several staff and parents who disagree about what a counselor should do in this situation. Some think he should never discuss it or just answer it in very simple terms and move on. One parent thinks if his child asks a question in front of a group, the counselor should answer it in front of the other campers. Another parent thinks we should change the subject and avoid the topic altogether. What are your thoughts?

One last thing is that some of the boys started to get a bit out of hand and tried to shock the counselor by asking explicit, graphic sexual questions.

Thanks in advance for your consideration of this delicate and puzzling issue.

— *D. M. Challenged in California*

Dear Challenged,

Your question is as perplexing to directors of non-Christian or secular camps as it is to you. I have heard from many camp directors about issues pertaining to sexual curiosity and camper sexual behavior. Your question is tough to answer in a general way because how one responds to talk about sex depends on many variables. However, it only seems fair to try to come up with some guidelines for counselors who are, after all, faced with camper situations like these "in the trenches" on a daily basis.

Guideline 1: Staff do not initiate discussions of sexuality.

Campers are certainly stimulated enough by elements in our society without having counselors add to it. This is another way of saying, "If it's not an issue, don't make it on." As you said in your letter, sex is not a topic counselors should bring up.

Guideline 2: Preempt talk about sex with talk about relationships.

One of the most basic tenets of behavior management is that children have an easier time refraining from unwanted behavior if we give them something else to do in its place. Teens and preteens, for example, are almost as curious about relationships as they are about sex. Counselors could easily have informal group discussions to talk about the qualities of healthy relationships. Doing so would help set expectations about what is appropriate to talk about publicly at camp by modeling it. The following issues are usually compelling ones for teens:

- how you can tell if a girl/boy likes you;
- what it means to respect the person you care about;
- having your own likes and dislikes separate from the one you care about;
- caring about someone does not mean being joined at the hip;
- a true loving relationship enhances the rest of your life and does not take you away from other people, your own interests, or aspects of your life;
- sex and love and love and affection are not synonymous; and
- seeing the person you care about for who they are and not who you need them to be.

I am certain that once such age-appropriate group discussions were started that other relevant topics would surface. If, in the course of such a discussion, some campers became provocative, and with some teens this is always a possibility when talking about heterosexual relationships, counselors would use guideline #4 below to handle it.

Guideline 3: Determine whether campers are being sincere or provocative.

How counselors respond to campers when it comes to talk about sex will largely be determined by this test. If, as you state in your letter, campers are trying to "shock the counselor" or are getting over-stimulated (e.g., silly or provocative), it is important to stop the discussion immediately. The first line of defense is to say, as calmly as possible, "You know that kind of talk is not okay here at camp." I stress the word "calmly" here because the more irate or defensive a counselor gets, the more satisfying it is to the camper provoking him (or her) and the more the camper will persist. If a camper says, as some have, that they talk this way all the time with their friends, the response should be, "What you talk about with your friends in private is your business, but here at camp it's not okay." If campers still cannot control their own behavior, the second step is to remove them from their audience or their audience from them. If they are still being provocative, arrange for them to call their parent (or, worse, their grandparent) and have them say over the phone what it was they were doing or saying. This technique has a deeply sobering effect on most campers. Obviously, such a call must be arranged with the knowledge and direction of the director.

Guideline 4: Provocative or graphic sex talk is simply unacceptable.

Allowing campers to continue being provocative or suggestive is not good for anyone involved. The quieter, less-assertive campers become embarrassed, uncomfortable, and feel unsafe in the presence of such behavior, while the more-provocative campers become increasingly unmanageable. It is also important for counselors to be made aware of the fact that persistent, provocative sexualized talk on the part of a particular camper may be a call for help. Children who have been a witness to or victim of inappropriate sexual behavior often signal their distress by being provocative. Likewise, children who are in danger of acting out sexually may signal their need for help by dropping hints through explicit sexual conversation. In either case, if counselors have any concerns about a camper, they should discuss them with a director who is in a better position to affect a helpful intervention.

Guideline 5: Counselors should not share their own experience when it comes to sex.

One of the most-common problems at camp is related to its very success. When counselors live in close quarters with campers and a trusting environment is created, there is a risk that the boundary between counselors and campers may become blurred. One way the boundary is blurred is when counselors share details of their own private romantic exploits with campers. There have been times at camp when campers have actually waited up for their counselor to come back from a day or night off out of their sheer curiosity. Again, staff need to be alerted and then supported throughout the summer regarding this understandable, yet unacceptable danger.

In some ways, camp may be the perfect place for children to get their information about relationships, of which sex is "the icing on the cake." Unfortunately, as Lynn Ponton points out in her book, *The Sex Lives of Teenagers* (Penguin Books, 2000), we are of two minds about sex in this country—on the one hand, it pervades our society; on the other hand, we sometimes pretend it is not there. Neither approach is helpful to children. At least at camp, they figure they might get to talk about it in a sensitive, respectful, nonprurient way.

Dear Bob,

I would like your opinion on the subject of male campers sitting on the laps of female counselors, and female campers sitting on the laps of male counselors. Should this be forbidden? Is it developmentally dangerous? I welcome your guidance.

— O.D.

Dear O.D.

First of all, let's talk about counselors of either gender having campers of either gender sit on their laps, since the potential for this to be over-stimulating or inappropriate is equal no matter which combination we are talking about. On the one hand, such behavior is the natural outcome of children feeling safe and comfortable with young adults they trust. On the other hand, I would, for the sake of maintaining that safety, have strict guidelines around lap sitting. First, it should always occur in the company of other adults. Second, the age of the camper is significant. Girls or boys under the age of nine sitting on the lap of a counselor of the opposite sex is acceptable. Girls or boys under the age of eleven sitting on the lap of a counselor of the same sex is acceptable. Third, except for certain special situations that are deliberately discussed with and decided on by a supervisor, I would discourage counselors from allowing campers who are not in their primary care (those from other cabins, bunks, or groups) to sit on their laps. There is more danger that lap sitting can become over-stimulating than there is any developmental danger, like extending or encouraging dependency in a child instead of encouraging independence.

20

Staff-to-Camper Communication Guidelines
by Bob Ditter

Dear Bob,

We have a veteran staff member who is excellent with children. He is a school guidance counselor known for his good work with students. He does not seem to have a strong peer group apart from the youth he spends time with, and he is constantly creating opportunities to befriend boys through the ski trips, concerts, church fellowships, and other outings he takes with them. He has on more than one occasion invited small groups of boys to stay over at his house, which has raised concern with parents that may or may not have been brought to the attention of the school.

What should our response be to the parent from his school who also has a connection to camp and has inquired about this staff member?

— *Concerned at Camp*

Dear Concerned,

The issue of staff contact with campers off-season is being raised by directors all over the country. With increased use of the Internet and instant messaging (IM), communication between campers and counselors has increased dramatically in the last few years, creating a need for a well thought-out policy or set of guidelines regarding this contact. I will respond to your specific question about your staff member and use it to address this broader concern.

The staff member you describe has some characteristics that raise my concern. Having what seems like stronger ties to boys than to his peers, coupled with what would appear to be a social-emotional life that centers on young boys, are both classic warning signs. You did not say whether he was married or in a relationship, but if he is single, it would only be another indicator that he has not developed a close, intimate bond with someone his own age.

Having highlighted these patterns, I hasten to add that none of these realities are evidence that he is doing anything inappropriate with the boys he spends time with. Everyone who enjoys working with youth gets a certain amount of emotional fulfillment from doing so. In the overall scheme of things, it is part of what ensures that children will get the care and attention they need from adults to thrive.

However, the man you describe has no apparent adult outlet for his intimacy needs, and away from camp (or school), there is not the structure or presence of other adults to keep things in balance. In this regard, this man is taking a risk in that he is leaving himself open to becoming emotionally over-involved with the boys whose company he keeps, which could result in hurt feelings, inappropriate intimate behavior (IIB), or an accusation, true or false, of an IIB. For these reasons, it is no surprise that several parents have been concerned about boys sleeping over at this man's house. At this point, I can hear my readers asking the same question that is on my mind, which is, where are the parents of the boys who are staying over? It seems to me their children's well-being is at some risk, a risk the parents must at least share, if they are being allowed to participate in these sleepovers.

You also never mentioned exactly what your camper parent's question was about this man, but let us assume it is a general question about his appropriateness with boys. What you will say is that he is great with kids and that you are lucky to have him at camp. You will add that you do not condone outings between staff members and campers outside of camp not so much, because you do not trust the people you hire, but because such outings do not have the built-in structure and safeguards of camp, which includes the presence of other campers and multiple adults. You might throw in the camper-to-staff ratio required by the American Camp Association Standards, which is a way of ensuring that proper supervision of children and adults is maintained, and that such a ratio would probably not be maintained once outside of the purview of camp. You might also say that as a general rule you do not recommend that parents allow their children to go on such outings, again because the kind of supervision or structure you have at camp would not be present. You will emphasize, of course, that this is the policy you have with regard to any staff member, not just this particular man.

The Internet Connection

Many camp professionals have spoken to me about their concerns of post-season communication and contact between campers and staff being fueled by the exchange of email and IM addresses at camp. Some of this contact may be very positive, as it helps keep the nourishing experiences campers have at camp alive and helps maintain their connection to camp.

However, as with any such communication, there is the challenge of oversight—one can never be exactly sure what is being communicated or whether that communication is appropriate. I would not always count on campers to tell their parents if the communication became inappropriate. For this reason, I recommend that email exchanges between campers and staff be allowed only with the awareness and approval of the camper's parents. I suggest this policy be communicated to the staff both at the beginning of the summer and several days before the end of each session. I suggest campers and camper parents be informed of this policy both before and after camp. What you say is that you handpick your staff and you stand by their ability to care properly for campers—in camp. That outside camp you cannot guarantee that the kind of supervision, oversight, or program structure will be present. Parents should also be made to understand that staff members do not represent camp once the season is over (unless, of course, they are full-time employees of the camp doing camp business).

Shift the Burden

What I am doing with this policy is shifting the burden of responsibility and oversight of campers back to their parents. If parents wish to allow their children to have contact with camp staff after camp, whether by email or in person, you cannot stop them. However, you can make it clear that they, not you, are then responsible for whatever occurs as a result. You, after all, have no way of knowing how the relationship between a staff member and a camper will develop outside of camp.

Sensible Guidelines

As in the case of your veteran staff member, if parents do decide to allow their children to see or have contact with camp staff outside of camp, you might, after clarifying that parents do so against your advice, suggest they at least follow some guidelines in such instances. Those guidelines would include no one-on-one outings between a child and an adult. In other words, other people should be included in any such outing, preferably another adult.

It would also be inadvisable for a child to sleep over at a staff member's house, and if a staff member were invited by the family to stay at the home of a camper, he or she should be in a separate room and not with the child. In the case of the boys from school staying at their guidance counselor's home, those parents (and the guidance counselor himself) are taking a risk. At minimum, there should be other adults present, and the boys should sleep in a room separate from the adults. It should also be made clear that by recommending these guidelines, which is optional on your part, you are not implying in any way that you or camp then takes responsibility for whatever does or does not happen.

The safety of campers is and should be a top priority for all camp professionals—one in which camper parents share.

21

Taking Stock—Best Practices for Even Better Summers

by Bob Ditter

Fall is the season when camp professionals experience their greatest differences. While some jump right from summer camp into the so-called "shoulder season," hosting school groups, sports teams, and weekend outings, others are wrapping up the summer with parent/camper surveys, filling orders for pictures from the Web, or making plans for a vacation before starting in on the next season. Directors of nonprofit camps, who often switch back to their off-season duties, quickly get caught up in the daily demands of their sponsoring centers. Whatever your focus this September, take time to reflect on the previous summer while it is fresh in your mind. This reflection will provide some rich material for next summer's training and steer you toward best practices in your year-round camp work.

Start With Inspiration

One of the aspects of camp most of us love to talk about is the way we so often make a difference in the lives of both campers and staff. This is echoed by staff, who consistently cite their desire to "make a difference" in the life of a child/lives of children as the number one factor motivating them at camp. Seldom, however, do camp professionals, as a regular practice, document in some colorful, accurate, detailed way those success stories of the summer to share with the staff the following year. Wouldn't it make sense to write down some of your success stories and breakthroughs now while you can remember the nuances and details of your success?

Create a book of best practices

What were your success stories for the past summer? What campers had breakthroughs, large and small? What staff members overcame obstacles to "step up to the plate?" Get a notebook, title it your "best practices" book, and write out some of those tales. Send an email out to staff this fall, especially to your "best performers," asking for their stories (if you didn't have the chance to survey them before they left at the end of the summer) or to supply you with details to your own recollections. Remind yourself to begin your staff orientation next summer with these human-interest narratives. Doing so has a much-greater impact on your staff at the opening of orientation than reciting your "camp philosophy." As I tell camp professionals everywhere, if you run your orientation well, your staff will be able to tell you what your philosophy is at the end of orientation just from the way they have been greeted and dealt with during staff training.

Identify New Allies

Every summer has its heroes—staff who truly rise to the top and become incredible performers; parents of new campers who are now "true believers" because their children got so much more from camp than they ever expected; and campers who surprise us all and achieve more than we thought possible. Make a list of your new and true allies, because they can help you continue to deliver the best camp experience possible.

Partner with parents

Cultivate a relationship with parents who are especially happy with camp or who are particularly satisfied about something special they or their children received from you or your staff. These parents can help you identify other families that might be interested in your camp, or they may be willing to host small gatherings for you when you come to their neighborhood to give a slideshow/video presentation about camp to prospective families. You might consider inviting a small, select group of parents to orientation to speak with your staff about what they want for their children, about the kind of care they are looking for, about any advice they have for staff about their children, etc. Parents who feel distinctly grateful for the experience or service they or their children received this summer are perhaps your best candidates for your panel next summer. If you have not invited parents to camp for orientation yet, I can only tell you that every camp director I have spoken to who has done this has told me how powerful and inspiring these presentations were for both the staff and the parents involved.

Identify top performing staff

As far as staff are concerned, establish an ongoing relationship with those staff you feel are truly your best performers. The Internet makes this easier than ever to do, and as most of us have seen, staff that do not respond to phone messages or regular (snail) mail do respond to email. Ask your top performing staff to host a small gathering at their schools later in the year (which you or your designated alternative attend) to help you recruit new staff. Counselors who are truly strong performers will recommend camp to their friends in a personal way that you simply cannot match, and they will recommend it only to those individuals whom they think can "cut it" at camp. According to results from a 2000 survey of twenty camps throughout the United States, staff who were personally referred by certain other staff (your best performers) were rated very high in terms of their own performance during the summer.

Turn your campers into writers

In terms of campers you identify as having had an exceptional summer, have them write a small story for your website about their experience. Some campers will be thrilled to see their own piece on your website, and doing this can only enhance the bond of loyalty that camper family has with you.

Best Practices

Before the summer gets too far away from you, write down the little things that happened during orientation that seemed particularly effective. For example, several camps bring their first-time staff in to camp anywhere from 24-36 hours before returning staff. This gives them a chance to get settled and become familiar with the place before all the old-timers come in. It also gives your international staff a chance to adjust to the time change, jet lag, and some of the customs. Other camps have a "warm fuzzy" meeting with their staff early in orientation. During the meeting, each staff member decorates a paper bag with their name and any special design. Other staff members drop appreciative notes or memos of congratulations in the bag during orientation. It is just a way for staff to acknowledge the contributions of one another. What other practices, either from orientation or from the summer itself, are ones you want to make sure you repeat next year? What glitches and mistakes do you want to make sure you avoid or account for next year? All of these observations should go into your "best practices" book, which you should also then circulate among your trusted key staff for their ideas and recollections. Looking back at it next May, when you will once again be "gearing up" for the coming summer, you will be glad you took the time to gather your notes this fall.

22

The Parent Factor

by Bob Ditter

These days, any discussion about camper behavior is incomplete without careful consideration of the parents—specifically, when and how often to call them; how, if at all, to involve them in the process of their child's adjustment to camp; and what to do if they have a negative reaction to any less than flattering news about their child. The relationship parents have with their children today and the ramifications this has for people working with them is sufficiently complex enough to need its own forum. In fact, parents are so involved with and worried about their children that any response to camper behavior should, as a matter of course, include some thought about what I call "the parent factor."

Defining the Parent Factor

When you take the potential influence parents can have on their child's attitudes and combine it with the trust they have in you and your program, you have the parent factor. It is crucial to take the parent factor into account when addressing camper behavior, because how parents work with you or against you has everything to do with how successful you are going to be with their children. A parent who doesn't trust you or give you the benefit of the doubt when a problem arises may align himself or herself against you and undermine your good efforts. I recall a camp parent a few years ago who, after hearing that the camp had decided to handle her daughter's rude and offensive behavior toward other girls by preventing her from going to a coed camp "mixer," called saying she had polled her friends and they all agreed that the camp's response was "inappropriate." "The 'vote' was decisive." the mother exclaimed. She and her friends had determined that her daughter should not have to suffer the deprivation of missing this highly anticipated social event. (The camp director responded by saying he was sure that when she and her husband addressed their children's misbehavior at home, they didn't poll the neighborhood first to get agreement.)

Dealing With Anxious Parents

Years ago, the parent factor did not loom so large in the life of camp professionals. Back then the prevailing attitude among camp professionals toward parents was something like, "Give us your child, get out of our way, trust us to do what we do well, and your child will be better for it." Parents were, by and large, not as demanding, not as involved, not as worried as parents today. These days, parents plant cell phones on their children and instruct them to call them if they have a problem. These days, parents scan the camp photo galleries on the Web scrutinizing their children's faces for any perceived sign of discomfort or ailment. One camp mother developed a "secret sign" with her sons that they were instructed to flash in camp photographs to indicate how they were doing—a sort of "thumbs up, thumbs down" ways of their letting her know whether she could relax because everything was okay or whether she should speed-dial camp and find out what was wrong. Some parents are so protective of their children that one-day camp director recently reported a mother who insisted on coming to camp everyday to hold a towel up for her young daughter who was too shy and embarrassed to change for pool time in front of other children.

What accounts for this worried, over-protective effort on the part of so many parents to manipulate their children's world? Wendy Mogel, in her book, The Blessing of a Skinned Knee, gives us some clues. She suggests that parents, constantly barraged by dreadful news from a media intent on playing on our fears, are anxious about preparing their children to live in a world with such a seemingly uncertain future. Parents look to give their children every advantage, every extra "edge," and work hard to build up their children's self-esteem, a way to buttress them against the setbacks of a cruel and fateful world, by telling them that everything they do and say is special and exceptional. Unfortunately, the effect is that children are both pampered and over protected, resulting in their being at once demanding and unable to cope.

Responding to Parents

So how, practically speaking, do camp professionals respond to parents today? First, remember that you build your reputation with parents over time, one interaction at a time. The phrase I have always used for this is "money in the bank." Not only do we make deposits into the "accounts" of campers, we do it with parents, too. Parents talk to one another. When they do, they create a "buzz." The buzz you want to create is that you are honest, knowledgeable about kids, a good listener, and careful and thoughtful in your dealings with people. You don't even need to create this buzz with all your parents, just a critical mass. It is your good reputation ("They got back to me right away.") and it is your attentiveness to detail ("They called us after the kids arrived to tell us they were okay.") that sustains you when you have an especially challenging parent situation.

Second, you need to keep parents better informed. Parents tell me that when a camp director or teacher calls, they don't want to feel as if their child is being judged, especially if their child has been exhibiting poor behavior. Parents feel responsible for their children's behavior and become defensive as it is. Keep your voice and your approach neutral and focused on solving the problem, not on blaming. Parents also want to know the truth, delivered compassionately, and what it is specifically you want from them. Do you simply want to keep them informed? Do you need their help in sorting out possible responses? Remember that parents, if surprised by their child's behavior, may want to figure out why. While interesting, it is usually more productive to figure out what will help. What have they tried in the past? Knowing their child, what approach might work best? Would it be helpful for parents to get on the phone and back you up?

Last, don't spend too much time on what Dr. Mogel calls the "lunatic fringe." The mother who insists on coming into day camp and holding that towel up for her daughter needs a firm, clear, and calm "no." If she leaves, there will be several other parents who go, "thank goodness you took a stand with her." Don't let the unreasonable antics of a few parents color your entire outlook on parents in general.

One last note: I have always found that, once parents sense my compassion and personal interest in their child, they want my help. Parents, regardless of what it may seem, want allies. If you come from the mindset that parents are a bother, it will make you less effective. If you can put yourself in parents' shoes and sense their uncertainty, it will help you fashion responses that are not only more successful, but will add to your reputation as a fair, reasonable, compassionate professional. Isn't that the kind of adult you would want to entrust with your child?

23

Working with Camper Parents
by Bob Ditter

Dear Bob,

I had a run in with a camper parent last summer that made me very uncomfortable. We have a visiting day for parents once each session, which, as you might imagine, is a stressful day for campers, parents, and staff all around. During the early afternoon, a parent who was demanding to know why her 15-year old son wanted to go home accosted me. I tried to reason with her, but she caught me off guard, and I felt awkward discussing this in the open with other parents and campers around.

Part of her complaint was, she had told me, her son had trouble making friends and he needed a lot of support to come to camp and be with boys his own age—boys who were essentially strangers to him. I repeated to her what I had said when we first spoke about "Jared" (not his real name) before camp. I told her that while we would do everything we could to help Jared find activities that he liked and help him get to know his new cabin mates, part of the work was up to him. His mother did not seem to hear what I was saying. It was as if she had her complaint, and nothing I said registered.

It seems to me, Bob, some parents want camp to make up for all the deficiencies or inabilities their children may have had for years. Help!

— *Simply Frustrated*

Dear Frustrated,

The noise you just heard was the sigh coming from hundreds of camp directors around the country who can relate only too well to your letter. Whereas staff issues used to be highest on the list of camp director concerns, parents are coming up fast. The topic of camper parents is too big to cover adequately in one sitting, but there are some general trends and pointers that may be useful. Let me talk a little about parents in general; then give you my thoughts about the situation you describe.

Though there are parents who are entitled and out to get whatever they can for their children with no regard to the rules or needs of others, most parents are, to borrow from you, "simply overwhelmed." Parents of a 15-year old boy said to me in my office just last night, "So much has changed since we were teenagers. We're sure Kieran (their son—also not his real name) has seen X-rated videos; we know he's looking at pornography on the Internet; he tells us that his friend, Jon, is sleeping with his girlfriend; and though we do not allow him to watch things like the Sopranos or Sex in the City, we discovered that his friends tape it for him. Not only that, but some of his best friends from camp were in town last weekend and Kieran came in smelling like pot. We love that he finally has these friends—he has been a loner for so long—but we're not happy about his smoking dope. We don't know what to do."

What Kieran's parents shared with me is both typical and the tip of the iceberg. Some parents do worry too much about their children. On the other hand, reading the news today, many parents feel helpless about protecting their children from the dangers of the world. I would say that an increasing number of parents send their children to camp partly as a way of getting them out of mainstream culture and into a place where they are sheltered and well supervised. Indeed, one of the reasons parents react so strongly to any news that suggests their child isn't doing well at camp is because they have their heart set on camp being that refuge and safe place. This is a tall order for directors to fill.

That having been said, minimizing parent concerns or trying to speak rationally before we have addressed the feelings involved does not work. Let's take the situation you describe. Realizing that you were taken off balance by the sudden outburst of this parent, the first goal should be to regain your footing. The best thing would be to say to this parent, "Look, this is important. Let's go someplace where we can sit down and really talk about what's going on. I want to be able to give this my full attention."

Making this move does several things at once. First, it creates a break in the action. This will allow you to regain your footing and this mother to calm down. Second, it takes the discussion into a private place where you both will be less distracted, and you can be more thoughtful about your responses.

Given that I was not present for your conversation, I cannot tell what you said and what you did not say. If you are like most directors when they are confronted by upset parents, you probably fall immediately into explaining or defending. What might be more effective is simply to acknowledge how concerned or worried she is about her son's difficulties and how tough it must be to watch him struggle. As I have often said to camp professionals, parents lead with their solution or complaint. This means they come across as demanding or angry, when underneath it all they are probably frightened and concerned. If we respond too quickly to their complaint or proposed solution, we may miss the opportunity to establish a more meaningful conversation about their child. Once parents have had their deeper concerns acknowledged, they are often more inclined to hear your ideas about what might or might not work.

Your letter reminds me of a somewhat different situation that a camp director in New York once told me about concerning a 15-year old boy who had a tendency to let his parents and other adults take more responsibility for his life than he seemed willing to do. During parent visiting day, the boy's mother came up to the camp director complaining about how her son's bunk was such a mess and his stuff so disorganized that he kept losing his things that were then costing her money. The camp director became defensive, talking about all they had tried to do to help "Jake" keep track of his things.

I suggested a different approach. I told the director to make himself "wrong." It might sound like, "You know, you're right. I think we did make a mistake. I don't think we realized how big a problem Jake has taking responsibility for his own stuff. We've all been working so hard at helping him keep track of his things that we're not giving him a chance to step up to the plate or suffer any consequences from being so messy. Let's talk about how we can change that right now."

While it might sound as if all you are saying is, "Jake needs to take more responsibility," saying it by making yourself "wrong" and making the parent "right" actually creates greater listening on the part of the parent. This allows you to get more of your message across.

About the American Camp Association

The American Camp Association (ACA) is a community of camp professionals dedicated to ensuring the high quality of camp programs, a greater public understanding of and support for the value of the camp experience, and an increase in the number of children, youth, and adults of all social, cultural, and economic groups who participate in the camp experience. Established in 1910, ACA operates as a private, nonprofit educational organization with members in all 50 states and several foreign countries. Its members represent a diverse constituency of camp owners and directors, executives, educators, clergy, businesses, consultants, camp and organization staff members, volunteers, students, retirees, and other individuals associated with the operation of camps for children and adults.